MW00977193

God Reveals His Decrees

compiled and condensed in good faith

paraphrased with fear of the Lord

from the written record of

Venerable Sister Mary of Agreda

published in 1657 in the voluminous books

"Ciudad de Dios" edited by M. DiMaio

for easy reading and public comprehension

First Edition

© copyright 2018

ISBN-13: 978-1723014147
ISBN-10: 1723014141

Description

The Almighty God in the Blessed Trinity had no beginning and has no end, the Alpha and the Omega. The Eternal Father, who knows all things, with His infinite wisdom and infinite knowledge knew the greatest love that could ever be is the love between a human mother and her child and the love of a human child for his mother. Knowing this the All-powerful God's greatest desire was to have this great love for Himself. As such, He would have to create a 'perfect mother' and He would have to become incarnate and born to this mother, thus creating the ideal circumstances for the Almighty God to experience the 'most perfect love'. From this concept in the Eternal Mind of God is the beginning and foundation of all creation. Thus, all creation derives its existence and purpose from this first concept in the Mind of God. Therefore, the Onlybegotten Son of the Father, Jesus, the 'perfect man' and the 'perfect woman' the Blessed Virgin Mary had their beginnings before the angels, the physical universe, and all of humanity.

The four Evangelists were not present when God sent His Archangel Gabriel to the Blessed Virgin Mary in Nazareth. The four Evangelists were not present when the Blessed Virgin Mary went and visited her cousin Elisabeth. The four Evangelists were not present, when Jesus was born, circumcised, visited by the Magi, or when the Holy Family fled to Egypt and many other events. It is obvious that the Blessed Virgin Mary had to have been the four Evangelists' primary source of information for the first chapters of the Gospel. Because of the Blessed Virgin Mary's great humility, she omitted a significant amount of information regarding herself and the Holy Family. In 1622 the Most High God decided and commanded the Blessed Virgin Mary to reveal all of the details of her life to the world.

i

This was accomplished by selecting the very holy devout Sister Mary of Agreda Spain to record and publish: the words of the Most High God Himself, the words of the Archangel St. Michael, the words of the Blessed Virgin Mary, and the words of two of her holy Angels.

And since everything comes into existence from her beginning as an idea and then as a reality, the entire story of creation would have to be told as well as the story of redemption and through the early years of the church. The collection of these recorded words were entitled "Ciudad de Dios" e.g. "City of God" which is a reference or another title given to the Blessed Virgin Mary. As such, the enormous impact could possibly be overlooked by the ambiguous title. For this reason the editor chose a title that would be hard to overlook; a title that would get attention and arouse curiosity. With no intention of disrespect or to diminish any aspect of "Ciudad de Dios", the editor compiled, condensed and paraphrased in order to compose and retell many of the stories in a format that would be easy to read and comprehend. The editor's rationale is that 200 pages of simple and easy to read material could be accomplished in a week, as compared to the highly spiritual detailed narratives consisting of 2,676 pages that can require several months to read, study and comprehend. And in the original format many readers become discouraged very early on and quit.

The goal of the editor by this reduced composition under the title of "God Reveals His Decrees" is to excite the reader with the most magnificent stories ever told, and should inspire the curiosity of individuals possessing higher intelligence to read and study the entire voluminous record contained in "Ciudad de Dios".

As the Bible is the most published and read book in the history of the world, then for the same reasons "Ciudad de Deus" should be the second most published and read text in history. The purpose of this book "God Reveals His Decrees" is to excite the readers and inspire their curiosity to learn more. In the Baltimore Catechism one of the very first questions is "Why did God make me?" The answer provided is that "God made us to know Him, to love Him, and to serve Him." As God's first command for mankind is "… to know Him.", then a good first start would be to read this book. All readers should come away with a greater love for the Most High God.

Dedicated to

**The Most High Tender Loving God
and His Tender Loving Blessed Mother**

For the conversion of sinners + salvation of souls, the enlightenment of the faithful.

The primary authors are:

**The Most High God, St. Michael the Archangel,
and The Blessed Virgin Mary**

In 1622 by the Most High's Decree dictated to and recorded by Sister Mary of Agreda.
Published in 1657 in Spanish under the title of "Ciudad de Dios"
English translation in 1902 by Fiscar Marison
aka Rev. George J. Blatter.

Introduction:
"Ciudad de Dios" has multiple imprimaturs and has been blest by 12 Popes. Pope Paul the VI stated that the texts did not have any content that is contrary to the teaching of the Catholic Church. The voluminous texts are the words of the Most High God, St. Michael the Archangel, the Blessed Virgin Mary and two of her Angels. Their words were dictated to Sister Mary of Agreda from 1622 to 1657.

The editor's objective is to condense 2,676 pages and to simplify highly complex narratives for easy reading of the most magnificent details described from the beginning of creation through the period of the Early Church that in many instances far exceed their abbreviated biblical counterparts. As biblical references are very well known, the editor has chosen to elaborate on details unknown to the vast majority that are revealed in "Ciudad de Dios" with the deliberate purpose of brevity and simplicity in order to hold the reader's interest for a few hours.

From the editor's experience, "Volume I - Conception" is the most difficult to read because of human mental limitations and inabilities to grasp highly spiritual detailed descriptions. Consequently, even his second and third readings took an exhausting 2 months for each reading. However, reading Volumes II, III, and IV, which are written with less spiritual terminology and familiar physical words, it was much easier to understand and was read in less than 4 weeks per volume. For some excellent readers the entire collection could be read and comprehended in perhaps less than 3 months, while most others might take 6 months or more. Because reading and studying "Ciudad de Dios" is so exhausting and laborious, many readers become discouraged and quit early on. For these reasons, the editor has reduced weeks of reading required for comprehending 2,676 pages, to a reading effort of 185 pages that could be easily accomplished in less than a week.

Contents

1. Creation

In "Ciudad de Dios" God's plan for creation progresses by Divine Decrees that are classified according to 6 Instants at which God took specific action.

1st Instant: God recognizes His infinite generosity.
2nd Instant: God would make Himself known.
3rd Instant: God determines the order of creation.
4th Instant: Jesus and Mary came first in the mind of God.
5th Instant: Creation of the Angels.
6th Instant: Creation of the human beings.

[Editor's caution: The explanation of the workings of the Intellect of the Most High God are beyond the capabilities of the finite human mind and therefore the written descriptions are extremely difficult to understand or interpret. In "Ciudad de Dios" Volume I – "Conception", this "Chapter 1, Creation is the most difficult to understand. Chapter 2, "The Battle for Heaven" is difficult but a little easier to comprehend. And from Chapter 3 on, the narratives become much easier to read and comprehend. The editor asks the reader to patiently persist.]

1st Instant [God's infinite generosity]
The first instant is: God recognizing His infinite attributes and perfections and the ineffable inclination to communicate Himself outwardly. This knowledge of God as being communicative *ad extra* comes first. God knowing His infinite attributes saw that it was just and proper, a duty and a necessity, to communicate Himself by exercising His generosity and mercy, by distributing outside of Himself His infinite treasures. God's determination to distribute His gifts and graces does not diminish His riches, but increases the inexhaustible fountain of His riches.

God foresaw this in the first instant after the communication *ad intra* by means of the eternal emanations. Seeing this He was obliged, to Himself, to communicate Himself *ad extra*, perceiving that He was holy, just, merciful, and god-like to do so; hence nothing could impede Him. God is not satisfied nor at rest with Himself until He reached the object of His desires, the creatures, where and with whom, by making them partakers of His divinity and perfections, He seeks His delight. In this enlightenment and knowledge there first is the inclination and urgent desire of God, and His strong will, to communicate His Divinity and the treasures of His grace. The second is the incomprehensible immensity of His good gifts, which He wishes to distribute according to this decree, assigning them for this purpose and yet remaining infinite, as if He had given nothing. This desire and inclination fills the Most High to sanctify, justify, overwhelm with gifts and perfections all creatures together and each one in particular for itself; provided these creatures would dispose themselves and place no obstacle toward receiving them.

2nd Instant [How God would make Himself known]
The second instant was to confirm and determine the object and intention of His communication of the Divinity *ad extra*, for His greater glory and to manifest Him as the Most High. God saw how He would communicate Himself, to make Himself known by His generosity in the distribution of His attributes, and set in motion His Omnipotence in order that He might be known, loved, praised and glorified.

3rd Instant [The order of creation]
The third instant consisted in selecting and determining the order and arrangement of His communication. The proper order should be maintained in regard to communications of God and His gifts so that the Almighty may execute in perfect sequence, harmony and subordination. In this instant was decreed first of all, that the Divine Word the second Person of the Blessed Trinity would assume flesh and would become visible. The perfection and the composition of the humanity of Jesus Christ our Lord was decreed and modeled in the Mind of the Most High God. Then were formed the ideals of the rest of men in imitation of the First, Jesus Christ. God prearranged that human nature be composed of an organic body and an immortal soul, endowed with faculties to know and enjoy its Creator, to discern between good and evil, and with a free will to love that same God.

This hypostatic union of the second Person of the Most Holy Trinity was necessary to have been the first object because before everything the Almighty issued *ad extra*.

One reason is God, having in Himself known and loved Himself, according to right order, know and love that, which approaches intimately to His Divinity, as is the case in the hypostatic union. Another reason is God having communicated Himself *ad intra*, should also communicate Himself *ad extra*; for this His works would be executed in perfect order. For God alone could be equitable in this operation. It was fitting that if God creates many creatures, He should create them in such perfect harmony. In conformity, all of His creatures must be subject to Him their Creator, to have communication and connection with His Divinity. For these reasons, the dignity of the works of God could be provided for only by the Incarnation of the Word and through Him creation should possess perfect order, which without Him was impossible.

4th Instant [Jesus & Mary came first in the mind of God]
The fourth instant was to determine the gifts and graces for the humanity of Jesus Christ our Lord, in union with the Divinity. Here the Most High opened the generous hands of His Omnipotence and His other attributes, in order to enrich the humanity and the soul of Jesus Christ with the highest abundance of His gifts and graces. His gifts flowed toward the humanity of the Incarnate Word, communicating to Him all knowledge, the grace and goodness of which His soul was capable as true God and true man, and at the same time, the Lord of all creatures capable of grace and glory.

In this instant a natural sequence, according to the decree and predestination of the Mother of the Word Incarnate was ordained a pure creature before the creation of the angels. Thus, before all other creatures, the Blessed Virgin Mary was conceived by the Mind of the Most High God and was fitting for the excellent gifts of the humanity of her most holy Son. Perceiving this most holy and pure Creature formed and conceived in the Mind of God from the beginning and before all the ages, the Blessed Virgin Mary is and forever God's Master Piece as the Mother of God.

3

5th Instant   [Creation of the angels]

In this fifth instant or decree is the creation of the angelic nature which is more excellent and more like unto the spiritual being of the Divinity, and at the same time the division or arrangement of the angelic hosts into nine choirs and three hierarchies, was provided and decreed. As they are created first of all for the glory of God, to assist the Most High and to know and love Him, so secondly they are ordained to assist, glorify and honor, reverence and serve the Eternal Word made flesh, recognizing Him as their Sovereign Lord and honoring Him along with His Mother, the Blessed Virgin Mary, Queen of these same angels. This commission was given to these angels. In this instant, Jesus Christ earned for them by His infinite merits, present and foreseen, all the grace, which they were to receive for their salvation. He was constituted as their Lord and supreme King, of whom they would be subjects. Even if the number of angels had been infinite, the merits of Jesus Christ would be abundantly sufficient for their salvation. Also in the fifth instant is the predestination of the good angels and the condemnation of the bad angels. God saw by means of His infinite knowledge and wisdom, all the works of the good angels and of the bad angels and the propriety of predestinating, by their free will and by His merciful generosity, those angels that would obey and give honor to Him and those angels who would rise up against Him the Most High God in pride and disobedience on account of their disordered self-love. In the same instant was decreed the creation of the Empyrean Heaven, for the manifestation of His glory and the reward of the good; also the earth and other heavenly bodies for the other creatures; more over also in the center or depth of the earth, hell, for the punishment of the bad angels.

6th Instant   [Creation of humankind]

God created Adam and the human beings to be the congregation for the Incarnate Word.

In the sixth instant was decreed the creation of humankind a congregation of people for Christ, who was already formed in the divine mind and will, and according to whose image and likeness man was to be made, in order, that the Incarnate Word might find brethren, similar but inferior to Himself and a

4

people of His own nature, of whom He might be the Head. In this instant was determined the order of creation of the whole human race, which was to begin from one man and woman and propagate itself, until the Blessed Virgin and her Son should be born in the predestined order. Because of the merits of Christ, the graces and gifts were prearranged and just, if they would only preserve it. The fall of Adam was foreseen and in him that of all others, except of the Blessed Virgin, who did not enter into this decree. As a remedy, it was ordained that the most holy God-man should be capable of suffering. The predestined were chosen by free grace and the reprobates with exact justice. All that was convenient and necessary for the conservation of the human race and for obtaining the end of the Redemption and the Predestination, was preordained, without interfering with the free will of men; for such ordainment was more conformable to God's nature and to divine equity. There was no injustice done to them, for with free will they could sin, so also could they abstain from sin by means of grace and the light of reason. God violated the right of no one, since He has forsaken no one nor denied to any one that which is necessary. Since his law is written in the hearts of men, nobody is excused for not knowing and loving Him as the highest Good of all creation.

2. Battle for Heaven

In the Book of Genesis, God said, "Let there be light." And He separated the light into day and into night." The meaning is not only the creation of light and the creation of day and night but the creation of the angelic light e.g. angels. And the separation of the good angels from the bad angels. The Book of Revelation also referred to as the Book of the Apocalypse provides more details.

The literal version of the 12th Chapter of the Apocalypse is as follows:

"And a great sign appeared in heaven: A woman clothed with the sun and the moon under her feet, and on her head a crown of twelve stars. And being with child, she cried travailing in birth, and was in pain to be delivered.

And there was seen another sign in heaven; and behold a great red dragon having seven heads and ten horns; and on his head seven diadems. And his tail swept one third of the stars of heaven and cast them down to the earth and the dragon stood before the woman, who was ready to give birth; that, when she should be delivered, he might devour her son.

And she brought forth a man-child, who was to rule all nations with an iron rod; and her son was taken up to God, and to his throne. And the woman fled into the wilderness where she had a place prepared by God, that there they should feed her a thousand two hundred and sixty days.

And there was a great battle in heaven; Michael and his angels fought with the dragon and his angels. And the dragon and his angels prevailed not, neither was their place found any more in heaven. And the dragon was cast out, that old serpent, who is called the devil and Satan, who seduces the whole world; and he was cast unto the earth, and his angels were thrown down with him." And a loud voice was heard saying: "Now is come salvation and strength, and the kingdom of our God and the power of His Christ; because the accuser of our brethren is cast out who accused them before our God day and night."

6

The Archangel Michael and his Holy angels overcame the dragon and his demons by the blood of the Lamb and by the word of the testimony, and they loved not their lives unto death. Therefore rejoice, O heavens, and you that dwell therein. Woe to the earth and the sea, because the devil is come down unto you, having a great wrath and knowing that he has but a short time.

And when the dragon saw that he was cast down to the earth he persecuted the woman, who brought forth the man-child. And God gave to the woman two wings of a great eagle that she might fly into the desert to a place prepared for her, where she is protected for seven years from the dragon. And the dragon cast out of his mouth after the woman, water as if it were a river that he might cause her to be carried away by the river.

And the earth helped the woman and the earth opened its mouth and swallowed the river, which the dragon cast out of his mouth. And the dragon was angry against the woman and went to make war with the rest of her seed, who keep the commandments of God, and live by the testimony of Jesus Christ." "Ciudad de Dios" provides even greater detail and elaboration on what took place:

The third heaven, the highest heaven, the Empyrean Heaven was the dwelling place of the angels and not yet the dwelling place of God. Although all of the angels could communicate directly with God, there was a veil that kept the angels from beholding the Most High God in all of His glory.

God created the angels to exist with varying powers, abilities and spiritual beauty. The angels varied by different groups or "choirs". There were 9 different choirs. From greatest to least they are: Seraphim, Cherubim, Thrones, Dominions, Powers, Virtues, Principalities, Archangels, and Angels. To illustrate their differences, there was nothing that the Cherubim knew or could tell the Seraphim that the Seraphim didn't already know. There was nothing that the Thrones could tell the Cherubim that the Cherubim didn't already know. etc. etc. etc.

7

The greatest, most powerful and most beautiful of all of the angels that God created was one of the Seraphim and his name was Lucifer (which means "the bearer or bringer of light or knowledge").

After God created the angels, there was a probationary period, during which God gave them three commands to test their fidelity. The first command was "You must love the Most High God above all things. I alone must you obey and serve." All of the angels obeyed God's first command but for different reasons. Those angels that would remain loyal to God, obeyed out of grateful appreciation to their Creator for their creation; these angels realized that God had created them with great power, magnificent abilities, as beautiful spirits. And for all that God had done for them, these angels loved Him without reservation. The other angels, who would later become the devils, also obeyed and gave their love because they reasoned that they could never be greater than their Creator.

Then God gave all of the angels His second command: "I the Most High God will create a lesser nature than the spiritual nature of the Angels. This lesser nature will possess both a tangible physical body and a spiritual soul. Of this inferior nature of human beings, I will raise up a "perfect man" and you superior in nature angelic spirits will be submissive and serve the "perfect man". The loyal and holy angels immediately submitted and pledged their obedience to God's second command.

With great indignation Lucifer wielded his power and beauty before all of the angels in Heaven. And many followed his lead as he refused to obey God's second command. Lucifer blasphemed and cried out: "Unjust is God in raising the human nature above the angelic. I am the most exalted and beautiful angel and the triumph belongs to me. I will subject myself to no one of an inferior nature, and I will not consent that anyone take precedence over me or be greater than I." In the same way spoke the apostate angels of Lucifer.

8

Instantly thereupon, a courageous and loyal champion arose who is the Archangel Michael. Knowing that of himself, he could not overcome Lucifer but the Archangel Michael knew the Almighty God could give him the strength to defeat Lucifer. So he rushed to ask God for the power and permission to cast Lucifer and his defiant angels out of Heaven. But God said "No." And then He showed Lucifer and Lucifer's angels a vision of their punishment in hell for all eternity. Lucifer defiantly responded, "Better to reign in hell than to serve in heaven!"

Then God gave His third and final command: "I will create a 'perfect woman' that you angels must also submit to and serve." Again the holy angels submitted and pledged their obedience to God's third command. To the contrary, Lucifer and his supporters were more defiant and enraged at God's third command even more than at God's second command. Lucifer more defiant than before said to God, "This 'perfect man' that you will create, I will destroy. And the 'perfect woman' that you will create, I will crush."
Lucifer's words caused God to respond with great outrage and He said, "This Woman will crush your head and she will have power and authority over you."

The Archangel Michael immediately rushed a second time to ask God for the power and permission to cast Lucifer and his supporters out of Heaven. Again, God said, "No. Wait. Let me reveal more so that perhaps Lucifer and his angels may relent." Then God revealed to all of the angels, "The 'perfect man' will be Myself in the Second Person as the Incarnate Word. And He will be both God and man. God's holy angels respond with great joy and wonder at the humility of God and pledged their obedience to serve and love.

Confronting the arrogant pride of Lucifer, St. Michael, burning with zeal to defend the Throne of God and armed with his own humility, said:

"Worthy is the Highest of honor, praise and reverence, and of being loved, feared and obeyed by all creation. The Most High is mighty to work whatever He desires. He that is increate with no beginning and without dependence on any other being, cannot seek anything that is not most just. To us He gave grace such as we have, creating us and forming us out of nothing. He can create other beings, as many and in what manner He pleases. It is reasonable that we submit and prostrate in His presence, adore His Majesty and kingly grandeur. Come then, ye angels, follow me, let us adore Him, and extol His admirable and secret judgments, His most perfect and holy works. God is most exalted and above all creatures, and He would not be the Most High, if we could attain or comprehend His great works. Infinite He is in wisdom and goodness, rich in the treasures of His benefits. As Lord of all and needing none, He can distribute His gifts to whomsoever He wishes, and He cannot err in the selection. He can love and confer His favor to whomsoever He chooses, and He can love whom He likes; He can raise up, create and enrich according to His good pleasure. In all things He will be wise, holy and irresistible. Let us adore and thank Him for the wonderful work of the Incarnation which He has decreed, and for His favors to His people and for their restoration to grace should they fall. Let us adore this Person endowed with the human and the divine nature, let us reverence Him and accept Him as our Head; let us confess, that He is worthy of all glory, praise and magnificence, and, as the Author of grace, let us give Him glory and acknowledge His power and Divinity."

Lucifer proclaimed, "God is a fool to become a man and does not deserve to have dominion over us. Therefore, I Lucifer, the greatest of all the angels, shall raise my throne above the Throne of the Most High and all of the angels will submit and serve me."

As all of the heaven was shakened, St Michael rushes to the Throne of God for the third time with the same request. This time God granted his request.

10

Lucifer at the sight of the holy prince St Michael, not being able to resist, was torn with interior rage and sought to flee from his torments. It was the will of God, however, that he should not only be punished, but also conquered, in order that by his fall he might know the truth and power of God. Now this time, St. Michael full of zeal and armed with power of the Most High rushed with righteous indignation to engage Lucifer, and said to Lucifer, "You are not Lucifer the angelic. You are Satan the adversary. *Who is like unto my God?* Be silent, Satan, cease thy dreadful blasphemies, and since iniquity has taken possession of you, depart from our midst, wretch, and be hurled in thy blind ignorance and wickedness into the dark night and chaos of the infernal pains prepared for you in hell. Let us, O Angels of the Most High, honor and reverence this blessed Woman, who is to give human flesh to the Eternal Word; and let us recognize Her as our Queen and Lady."

The great sign of the "Woman clothed with the sun and a crown of twelve stars and the moon under her feet" served St Michael the Archangel and his Angels as a shield and as arms of battle against the devils; for at the sight of it, these demons with all their power of reasoning weakened were brought to confusion and silence, since they could not endure the mysteries and sacraments contained in this sign. And just as by divine power this mysterious sign appeared, so also now the other figure or sign of the dragon appeared, in order that thus transformed he might be ignominiously hurled from heaven amid the fright and terror of his followers and amid the astonishment of the holy angels. As Jesus told His disciples, "I saw Satan fall like lightning from the sky."

In the Empyrean Heaven a loud voice was heard saying: "Now is come salvation and strength, and the kingdom of our God and the power of His Christ; because the accuser of our brethren is cast forth, who accused them before our God day and night." This was the voice of the Word the Second Person of the Holy Trinity. As all of the Holy Angels joined in the loud cry, "Pater semprus et Dominum" "Father you are forever our Almighty God".

11

And God's veil was lifted and for the first time the Angels could see the Most High in all His splendor and glory. The Angels were happy to surrender their free wills and join their spirits with God in what is known as the Beatific Vision also known as the Communion of Saints. From that moment on the Holy Angels are incapable of committing sin or doing anything contrary to the Will of God. And the Empyrean Heaven became the dwelling place of the Most High God and His Holy Angels forever.

The loss of one third of God's angels caused great consternation. St. Michael wanting further to please God, asked for His permission to destroy the empty thrones and dwelling places vacated by Lucifer and his followers. God answered, "No. These places are reserved for and will now be given to all of the souls of humankind that will be saved by my Onlybegotten Son". In later chapters of "Ciudad de Dios", the Blessed Virgin Mary reveals that the throne of Lucifer was given to St. Francis of Assisi.

Recall the gospel, where Jesus says, "In my Father's house there are many dwelling places. ... I go now to prepare a place for you, so that where I am you may also be."

3. God chooses Joachim & Anne to be the Parents of Blessed Virgin Mary

After the fall of humankind, many generations had passed and the time had come for the Incarnate Word to take on flesh. Joachim and Anne were created by special decree according to the will of God.

St. Joachim had his home, his family and relations in Nazareth, a town of Galilee. In continual devout prayer he asked God to fulfill His promises. Joachim's faith and charity was noticed by God. He was humble, pure, sincere and honest.

St. Anne had a house in Bethlehem and was chaste, humble and beautiful. From childhood she led a virtuous, holy, simple life and was enlightened in prayerful contemplation. She was diligent and industrious, attaining perfection in both the active and the contemplative life. She was unequalled in the virtues of faith, hope and love. Her prayers were most acceptable to God and facilitated the coming of the Redeemer.

St. Anne prayed fervently that the Almighty would procure for her in matrimony an upright man. At the moment in which St. Anne prayed to God, St. Joachim made the same petition; both prayers were presented at the same time before the tribunal of the Holy Trinity, where they were heard and fulfilled that Joachim and Anne unite in marriage and become the parents of Her, who was to be the Mother of the Incarnate God. The Archangel Gabriel was sent to announce it to them both. To St. Anne he appeared in visible radiant human form, while she was engaged in prayer for the coming of the Savior of humankind. When she saw Gabriel she tried to prostrate herself in profound humility to reverence him; but Gabriel prevented her from bowing down to him, as she being destined to be the mother of Mary most holy, Mother of the Word Incarnate. God only informed Gabriel of this mystery when he was sent with this message. The other angels did not yet know of it, as this revelation, knowledge had been given directly from God only to the Archangel Gabriel.

Nevertheless Gabriel did not at this time make it known to St. Anne; but he said to her: "The Most High gives you His blessing, servant of God. His Majesty has heard your petitions and He wishes you to persevere in prayer for the coming of the Redeemer. It is His will, that you accept Joachim as your spouse, for he is upright and acceptable to God. In his company thou will be able to persevere in God's law and service. Continue your prayers and do not ask for anything else, for the Almighty will grant your requests. Continue to pray for the Redeemer for He is your salvation." Then Archangel Gabriel disappeared.

To St. Joachim the Archangel Gabriel did not appear in a physical manner, but he spoke to Joachim in his sleep as follows: "Joachim, you are blest by the right hand of the Most High! Persevere in your desires and live according to justice and perfection. It is the will of the Almighty, that you receive Anne as your spouse, to her I have visited with His blessing. Take care of her and honor her as a pledge to the Most High and give thanks to His Majesty, because He has placed her into your charge." St. Joachim immediately asked for the hand of the most chaste Anne, and in obedience to God, they married. But neither of them manifested to each other the secret of what had happened until several years later. The two holy spouses lived in Nazareth. With humility they practiced all virtues in their works, making themselves very acceptable and pleasing to the Most High. The rents and incomes of their estate they divided each year into three parts. The first one they offered to the temple of Jerusalem for the worship of the Lord; the second they distributed to the poor, and the third they retained for their sustenance. God increased their goods because of their generosity and charity.

They lived without quarrel or grudge. The humble Anne subjected herself in all things to the will of Joachim. Joachim with equal humility, sought to know the desires of Anne, confiding in her and was never deceived. Joachim honored his spouse and lavished his attention upon her.

Joachim and Anne lived twenty years without children. Among Jews this was the greatest disgrace. Because of this, they bore many insults from their neighbors and acquaintances. They prayed for a child and vowed that if God should give them a child, they would consecrate the child to His service in the temple of Jerusalem.

The prayers of Joachim and Anne reached the throne of the Holy Trinity, where they were accepted and the will of God was made known to the holy angels. The three Divine Persons spoke to the Holy Angels as follows: "We have decided, that the Person of the Word shall assume human flesh and that through Him all of humankind can have salvation. ... Above all We have Our eyes on Her, who is to be the chosen One, who is to be acceptable above all creatures and singled out for Our delight and pleasure; because She is to conceive the person of the Word in her womb and cloth Him with human flesh. Since there must be a beginning of this work, by which We shall manifest to the world the treasures of the Divinity, this shall be the acceptable and opportune time for its execution. Joachim and Anne have found grace in Our eyes; We look upon them with pleasure and shall enrich them with choice gifts and graces. They have been faithful and their souls are acceptable and pleasing before Us. Let Gabriel, our ambassador, bring tidings of joy for them and the whole human race that We have chosen them."

Thus the Most High instructed the Angels in regard to His will and decree. The holy Archangel Gabriel humbled himself before the Throne of the Blessed Trinity. From the Throne an intellectual voice proceeded, saying: "Gabriel, enlighten and console Joachim and Anne, Our servants, and tell them, that their prayers have come to Us. Promise them that Anne shall conceive a Daughter, to whom We give the name of MARY."

With this message the Archangel Gabriel descended from the Throne room of the Empyrean Heaven and appeared to Joachim, while he was in prayer, saying to him:

"Just and upright man, the Almighty from His Sovereign Throne has taken notice of your desires and has heard your prayers, and has made you most fortunate on earth. Your spouse Anne shall conceive and bear a Daughter, who will be blessed among women. The Eternal God, the Creator of all, sends me to you, because your works and alms have been acceptable. ... The Almighty wishes to enrich your family with a Daughter, whom Anne will conceive; the Most High Himself has chosen for Her the name of MARY. From her childhood let Her be consecrated to the temple, and in it to God, as you have promised. ... On account of the sterility of Anne Her conception shall be miraculous. Mary will be a Daughter wonderful in all her doings. Praise the Almighty God, Joachim, for this benefit and magnify Him, for in no other has He done such a thing. You will give thanks in the temple of Jerusalem and you will meet, at the Golden Gate, your spouse Anne, who is coming to the temple for the same purpose. Remember this marvelous message, for the Conception of this Child shall all heaven and earth rejoice."

All this happened to St. Joachim during his prolonged prayer and in a sleep for the purpose of receiving this message. St. Joachim awoke in great joy and he concealed within his heart this favor of God. He thanked the Most High for His inscrutable judgments. In order to do this more appropriately he went to the temple as he was commanded by the Archangel Gabriel.

In the meanwhile Anne prayed: "Most High King and God of all creation ... Is it possible, that the Most High should descend from His Holy Heaven? Is it possible, that He is to have a terrestrial Mother? What woman shall She be, that is so fortunate and blessed? Execute, O Lord, this decree: fulfill Thy divine benevolence!" In this prayer, St. Anne weighed all the discussions, which she had had with her guardian angel, who on many occasions, and now more openly than ever before, had manifested himself to her. The Almighty ordained, that the message of the Conception of His Holy Mother should be similar to the Incarnation. The Archangel Gabriel brought both messages.

16

The Archangel Gabriel appeared to St. Anne in radiant human form and said to her: "Anne, servant of God, I am Gabriel sent from the council of the Most High, who in His mercy looks upon the humble. The Lord has heard your prayers, ... If He delays answering their prayers, it is in order to give much more than they ask and desire. ... The humility, faith and the alms of Joachim and yourself have come before the Throne of the Most High and now He sends me, Gabriel His angel, in order to give you news full of joy. His Majesty chooses you to be the mother of Her who is to conceive and bring forth the Onlybegotten Son of the Father. You will bring forth a Daughter, who the Most High has chosen the name MARY. She shall be blessed among women and full of the Holy Spirit. ... Know also that I have announced to Joachim, that he shall have a Daughter who shall be blessed and fortunate; but he does not know, that she is to be the Mother of the Onlybegotten Son of the Father. Therefore you must guard this secret. Now go to the temple to give thanks to the Most High for having been so highly favored. In the Golden Gate thou shall meet Joachim, where you will confer with him about this tiding. You are especially blessed by God. ..."

Immediately St. Anne went to the temple of Jerusalem and met St. Joachim. Returning to their home they discussed the message from the Archangel Gabriel that God had promised a Daughter who should be most blessed. On this occasion they also told each other, how Gabriel, before their marriage had commanded each to accept the other that together they might serve God. This secret they had kept from each other for twenty years, until the same angel had promised them a Daughter. Again they made the vow to offer Her to the temple and that each year on this day they would come to the temple to offer special gifts, spend the day in thanksgiving and give alms. St. Anne never disclosed the secret, that her Daughter was to be the Mother of the Redeemer. Nor did Joachim during his life know any more than she was to be great. But in the last moments of life the Almighty made the secret known to him.

After the conception of the body of the Mother of the Incarnate Word and before creating her soul, God said to her: "Anne, my servant, I am the God of Abraham, Isaac and Jacob; My blessing and My eternal light is with you. Now I wish the person of the Eternal Word, to become man, to be born of a Woman, who shall be Mother, Virgin, pure, immaculate, and blessed above all creatures. Of Her, My only One will be born, and I make you Her mother." By these enlightenments, the Almighty prepared St. Anne for the Conception of her most holy Daughter, the Mother of God, the Blessed Virgin Mary.

4. Revelations by God to the Holy Angels concerning the Blessed Virgin Mary

i. The Immaculate Conception of the Blessed Virgin Mary is revealed to the Angels

[Editor's note: In 1622 the Most High God decrees the Immaculate Conception of the Blessed Virgin Mary, that no stain of the 'original sin' would be allowed to contaminate her most pure and holy soul at the moment of her conception. This dogma of faith was revealed to the hierarchy of the Catholic Church in 1657 with the publication of "Ciudad de Dios". But the Church did not officially decree it until 1830.]

For God there is no past or future, since He holds all things present to his divine and infinite mind and knows all by one simple act. The Most High God decrees of the creation of a Mother befitting and worthy of the Incarnation of the Word, for the fulfillment of His decree is inevitable. The opportune and pre-ordained time had arrived. In the tribunal of the Blessed Trinity the Most High God reveals to His holy angels saying:

"Now is the time to begin the work of Our pleasure and to call into existence that pure Creature and that soul, which is to find grace in Our eyes above all the rest. Let Us furnish Her with the richest gifts and let Us deposit in Her the great treasures of our grace. Since all others, whom We called into existence, have turned out ungrateful and rebellious to our wishes, frustrating Our intention and impeding by their own fault Our purpose, namely, that they conserve themselves in the happy state of their first parents, and since it is not proper, that Our will should be entirely frustrated, let Us create this Being with sanctity and perfection, so that the disorder of the first sin shall have no part in Her. Let Us create a soul according to our pleasure, a fruit of Our attributes, a marvel of Our infinite power, without touch or blemish of the sin of Adam. ...

… Let Us perfect a work which is the object of Our Omnipotence and a pattern of the perfection intended for Our children, and the finishing crown of creation. All have sinned in the free will of the first man; let Her be the sole creature in whom We restore and execute that which they lost in their sin. Let Her be a most special image and likeness of Our Divinity and let Her be in Our presence for all eternity the culmination of Our good will and pleasure. In Her We deposit all graces which We had destined for the angels and men, if they had remained in their original state. What they have lost We renew in this Creature and We will add to these gifts many others. Thus our first decree shall not be frustrated, but it shall be fulfilled in a higher manner through this Our chosen and only One. And since We assigned and prepared the most perfect of Our gifts for the creatures who have lost them, We will divert the stream of Our bounty to Her. We will set Her apart from the ordinary law, by which the rest of the mortals are brought into existence, for in Her the serpent shall have no part. I will descend from heaven into her womb and in it vest Myself from her substance with human nature."

" … The Word, which is to become man, being the Redeemer and Teacher of men, must lay the foundation of the most perfect law of grace, and must teach through it, that the father and mother are to be obeyed and honored as the secondary causes of the natural existence of man. The law is first to be fulfilled by the Divine Word by honoring Her as His chosen Mother, lavishing upon Her the most admirable, most holy and most excellent of all graces and gifts. Among these shall be that singular honor and blessing of not subjecting Her to our enemy, nor to his malice; and therefore She shall be free from the death of sin. On earth the Word shall have a Mother without a father, as in heaven He has a Father without a mother. ... At no time shall the dragon boast of being superior to the Woman, whom God will obey as His true Mother. This dignity of being free from sin is due to that of being Mother of the Word, and it is in itself even more estimable and useful. It is a greater good to be holy than to be only mother; but all sanctity and perfection is nevertheless due to the human flesh, from which He is to assume form, must be free from sin. ...

20

Since He is to redeem in it the sinners, He must not be under the necessity of redeeming His own flesh, like that of sinners. Being united to the Divinity, His humanity is to be the price of Redemption, wherefore it must before all be preserved from sin, and We have already foreseen and accepted the merits of the Word in this flesh and human nature. We wish that for all eternities the Word should be glorified through His Mother."

"She is to be a daughter of the first man; but in the order of grace She is to be singularly free and exempt from fault; and in the order of nature She is to be most perfect, and to be formed according to Our special providence. And since the Incarnate Word is to be the Teacher of humility and holiness and for this end is to endure labors, confounding the vanity and deceitful fallacies of mortals by choosing for Himself sufferings as the treasure most admirable in Our eyes, We wish that She, who is to be His Mother, experience the same labors and difficulties, that She be singularly distinguished in patience, admirable in sufferings, and that She, in union with the Onlybegotten Son, offer the acceptable sacrifices of sorrow to Us for her greater glory."

This was the decree which the three divine Persons made known to the holy angels. Manifestation by the Almighty to the angels on this occasion: "Now the time has arrived" added His Majesty, "which was resolved upon by Our Providence for bringing to light the Creature most pleasing and acceptable to Our eyes. That Creature, in whom the human nature is freed from its first sin, who is to crush the head of the serpent, who was typified by that singular sign, the Woman that appeared in the heavens in Our presence, and who is to clothe the Eternal Word with human flesh. The hour is at hand, so blessed for mortals, in which the treasures of Our Divinity are to open the gates of heaven. Let the rigor of Our justice be softened by the chastisements, which We have until now executed upon the mortals; let Our mercy be given; let the creatures be enriched, and let the Incarnate Word merit for them eternal glory."

"Now let the human race receive the Redeemer, the Teacher, the Brother and Friend, to be life for mortals, a medicine for the sick, a consoler for the sorrowful, a balsam for the wounded, a companion for those in difficulties. Let now the prophecies of Our servants and the promises made to them, that We would send a Savior to redeem them, be fulfilled. And in order that all may be executed according to Our good pleasure, and that We may give a beginning to the mystery hidden since the beginning of the world, We select for the formation of Our beloved Mary the womb of Our servant Anne. ... Mary's creation shall proceed according to the usual order but shall be different in the order of grace, according to this Decree of Our Almighty power."

"You already know how the ancient serpent, since he saw the sign of this marvelous Woman, attempts to circumvent all women, from the first one created, he persecutes all women expecting to find among them the One, who is to crush his head. When he shall encounter this most pure and spotless Creature, he shall find Her so holy that he will exert all his powers to persecute Her in pursuance of the concept which he forms of Her. But the arrogance of this dragon shall be greater than his powers; and it is Our will that you angels have particular charge of this Our holy City and tabernacle of the Incarnate Word, protecting, guarding, assisting and defending Her against Our enemies, and that you enlighten, strengthen and console Her with all due solicitude and reverence, as long as She shall be a wayfarer among the mortals."

At this proposal of the Most High, all the holy angels, prostrate before the Royal Throne of the Most Holy Trinity, avowed their prompt eagerness to obey the Divine mandate. Each one desired in holy emulation to be appointed, and offered himself for such a happy service; all of angels gave the Almighty praise and thanksgiving in new songs, because the hour had arrived for the fulfillment of that for which they had, with the most ardent desires, prayed for throughout many ages.

On this occasion that from the time of the great battle of St. Michael with the dragon and his allies, in which they were hurled into everlasting darkness while the angelic hosts of St. Michael remained victorious and confirmed in grace and glory, these holy spirits commenced immediately to pray for the fulfillment of the mysteries of the Incarnation of the Word, of which they became aware at that time. And they persevered in these often repeated prayers up to the hour in which God manifested to them the fulfillment of their desires and petitions.

The angels at this new revelation conceived an additional joy and obtained new accidental glory, and these angels spoke: "Most High and incomprehensible God and Lord, Thou art worthy of all reverence, praise and eternal glory; and we are Thy creatures and made according to Thy divine will. Send us, all-powerful God to execute Thy most wonderful works and mysteries, in order that in all things Thy most just pleasure may be fulfilled." In such terms of affection the angels of heaven acknowledged themselves as subjects; and if it had been possible, they desired to increase in purity and perfection in order to be more worthy guardians and servants of the Blessed Virgin Mary.

ii. God chooses 1,000 Angels to protect the Blessed Mary

Then the Most High chose and appointed those who were to be occupied in this exalted service (the guardianship of Mary) from each of the nine choirs of angels. He selected one hundred, being nine hundred in all. Moreover, He assigned twelve others who should in a special manner assist Mary in corporeal and visible forms; and they were to bear the emblems or escutcheons of the Redemption. These are the twelve Seraphim that are represented as the "crown of twelve stars." Besides these the Lord assigned eighteen other angels, selected from the highest ranks of the Seraphim, who were to ascend and descend by that mystical stairs of Jacob with the message of the Queen to His Majesty and those of the Most High to Her. Many times she sent them to the Eternal Father in order to be governed in all her actions by the Holy Spirit.

23

She did nothing except what pleased the Almighty, and His pleasures She sought even in most insignificant things. Whenever She was not instructed by a special enlightenment, She sent these holy angels to the Most High to signify her desire to do what was most pleasing to Him and to be informed of His pleasure.

In addition to all these holy angels the Almighty assigned and appointed seventy Seraphim, choosing them from the highest ranks and from those nearest to the Divinity, in order that they might communicate and converse with this Princess of heaven in the same way as they themselves converse with each other, and as the higher communicate with the lower ones. This was a privilege conferred upon the Mother of God because She was to be a wayfarer on earth with an inferior nature, though in dignity and grace, superior to all the seraphim. At one time when the Lord withdrew and hid Himself from Her for three days in the temple, these seventy seraphim consoled and enlightened her; to them She poured out the longings of her most ardent love and her anxieties in regard to her hidden Treasure. That there were seventy of these spirits, was for the number of years of her life, which was seventy and not sixty.

These mighty angels and captains were assigned as a guard of the Queen of heaven from among the highest orders of the angelic hierarchy; for these, in that ancient battle of the obedient spirits with the proud dragon, were as the armed champions of the God of all creation, encountering and overcoming Lucifer and all his devils with the sword of their virtue and of the Divine Word. Hence, because they distinguished themselves in that great battle and victory by their zeal for the honor of the Almighty, and had been valiant and skillful captains in the divine love, and as they so zealously defended the honor of their Most High God and of His most holy Mother, We reward them to be her guardians. Thus the Word assumes humanity conceived in the virginal chamber of Mary by her most pure blood.

24

The Blessed Virgin Mary's one thousand Angels:
100 Angels + 100 Archangels + 100 Principalities
100 Virtues + 100 Powers + 100 Dominions
100 Thrones + 100 Cherubim + 100 Seraphim
70 Seraphim for Her 70 years of life
18 Seraphim as Her special messengers to God
12 Seraphim 'crown of twelve stars' Her inner circle

Altogether a thousand angels were chosen and the Blessed Virgin Mary was abundantly fortified against the infernal legions.

Her invincible warriors were well organized with St. Michael, the Commander of the heavenly army. St. Michael was placed at their head, and although not always in the company of the Queen, he was nevertheless often near her and often showed himself to her. The Almighty destined him as a special ambassador of Jesus our Lord and to act in some of the mysteries as the defender of His most holy Mother. In a like manner the Archangel Gabriel was appointed to act as legate and minister of the Eternal Father in the doings of the Blessed Virgin Mary. Thus the Most Holy Trinity provided for the custody and the defense of the Mother of God.

All the appointments of the angels were a grace of the Almighty; that He observed, according to a certain measure, the laws of distributive justice. In His equity and providence He took account of the manner in which the holy angels acted and felt in regard to the mysteries revealed to them in the beginning concerning His most holy Mother.When these holy angels appeared in visible shape to the Mother of God, they bore devices or badges representing the different mysteries. Some of them showed the emblems of the Incarnation, others those of the Passion, others those of the Queen herself, and of her great dignity. But she did not immediately recognize these badges when they began to be shown to Her, for the Almighty had told all these holy angels not to make known to her that she was to be the Mother of His Onlybegotten Son until the hour appointed by His divine wisdom; yet at the same time always to converse with her about the sacraments and mysteries of the Incarnation and the Redemption, in order to excite her fervor and her prayers.

5. Birth and Childhood of the Blessed Virgin Mary

The birth of the Blessed Virgin Mary happened on the eighth day of September, fully nine months having elapsed since the Conception of her soul. St. Anne was prepared by an interior voice of the Lord, informing Her, that the hour of her parturition had come. Full of the joy of the Holy Spirit at this information, she prostrated herself before God and besought the assistance of his grace and his protection for a happy deliverance. Mary was born pure and stainless, beautiful and full of grace, thereby demonstrating, that She was free from the law and the tribute of sin. Although She was born substantially like other children, her birth was accompanied by such circumstances and conditions of grace, that it was the most wonderful and miraculous birth in all creation and will eternally redound to the praise of her Maker. At twelve o clock in the night this divine Luminary issued forth, dividing the night of the ancient Law and its pristine darkness from the new day of grace, which now was about to break into dawn. She was clothed, handled and dressed like other infants, though her soul dwelt in the Divinity; and She was treated as an infant, though She excelled all mortals and even all the angels in wisdom. Her mother, St. Anne did not allow Her to be touched by other hands than her own, but she herself wrapped Her in swaddling clothes: and in this Saint Anne was not hindered by her present state of childbirth; for she was free from the toils and labors, which other mothers usually endure in such circumstances. So then St. Anne received in her arms Her, who was her Daughter, but at the same time the most exquisite Treasure of all the universe, inferior only to God and superior to all other creatures.

On the eighth day after the birth of the great Queen, multitudes of most beautiful angels in splendid array descended from on high bearing an escutcheon on which the name of MARY was engraved and shone forth in great brilliancy. Appearing to the blessed mother Anne, they told her, that the name of her daughter was to be MARY, which name they had brought from heaven, and which divine Providence had selected and now ordained to be given to their child by Joachim and herself.

The St. Anne called for her husband and they conferred with each other about this disposition of God in regard to the name of their Daughter. The more than happy father accepted the name with joy and devout affection. They decided to call their relatives and a priest and then, with much solemnity and festivity, they imposed the name of MARY on their Child. The angels also celebrated this event with most sweet and ravishing music, which, however, was heard only by the mother and her most holy Daughter. Thus was the divine Princess named by the holy Trinity: in heaven, on the day of her nativity, and on earth, after eight days. This name was written in the list of other names, when her mother presented herself at the temple according to the law, as I will relate further on. This was the birth, like to which none had been before, and the like of which cannot again happen in mere creatures. This was the most blessed birth of which nature was capable, for by it an Infant came into existence, whose entrance into the world was not only free from all impurities of sin, but who was more pure and holy than the highest seraphim.

St. Joachim and St. Anne fulfilled their promise to God and took their Blessed Child Mary at the age of three to the Temple in Jerusalem to be consecrated to the Most High and left her there to serve and advance in knowledge under the charge of the holy woman Anna. The child Mary was an immense joy and delight to the Almighty God and so much so that a few days could not pass before God would take her up to the Empyrean Heaven to enjoy her presence for prolonged periods. One of Mary's angels would take on her appearance, as if she was in a restful state or at night time as if she was asleep. These occurrences were very frequent as she brought so much happiness to the Most High.

In addition to Blessed Mary's one thousand angels guarding and protecting her, the Almighty placed a protective shield around her two hundred yards in all directions. Should Lucifer or any of his demons attempt to approach her, as soon as they would breach God's protective shield they would immediately feel intense pain. This pain would intensify the closer Lucifer would come. The pain was so intense that Lucifer could only withstand it for a few moments.

6. Annunciation & Incarnation

The Most High resolved to send His Onlybegotten Son into the
world to be raised and brought forth by the most holy Mary.
To facilitate this the Most High spoke to the Archangel Gabriel
in the way He was accustomed to intimating His will to the
holy angels. God usually illumines the holy spirits by
conversing with the higher angels, who in turn purify and
illumine the others in their order down to the least among
them, thus making known the revelations of the Divinity. Yet
on this occasion this usage was not maintained, for the holy
Archangel Gabriel received his message immediately from the
mouth of God.

At the bidding of the Almighty the Archangel Gabriel
presented himself at the foot of the Throne of the Most High.
Then the Almighty charged Gabriel with the message, that he
was to bring to the Blessed Virgin Mary and instructed him in
the very words with which he was to salute and address Her.
Thus the first Author of the message was God himself, who
formed the exact words in His Divine Mind, and revealed them
to the Archangel Gabriel for his announcement to the Blessed
Virgin Mary. The Blessed Trinity commanded Gabriel to take
himself directly to the Blessed Virgin Mary and announce to
Her, that the Most High had chosen Her among women to be
the Mother of the Eternal Word, that She should conceive Him
in her virginal womb through operation of the Holy Spirit
without injury to her virginity. In this and in all the rest of the
message, the Archangel Gabriel was instructed by the Blessed
Trinity Itself.

Thereupon the Most High announced to all the other angels
that the time of the Redemption had come and that He had
commanded it to be brought to the world without delay; for
already, in their own presence, the most holy Mary had been
prepared and adorned to be His Mother, and had been exalted
to the supreme dignity. The holy angels heard the voice of
their Creator, and with incomparable joy and thanksgiving for
the fulfillment of His eternal and perfect will, they sang new
canticles of praise, repeating therein that hymn of Sion:

28

"Holy, holy, holy art thou, God and Lord Sabaoth (Is. 6, 3). Just and powerful art Thou, Lord our God, who lives in the highest (Ps. 112, 5) and looks upon the lowly of the earth. Admirable are all Thy works, Most High and exalted in Thy designs."

The Archangel Gabriel, obeying with singular delight the divine command and accompanied by many thousands of most beautiful angels in visible forms, descended from the Empyrean Heaven. The appearance of the great prince and legate was that of a most handsome youth of rarest beauty; his face emitted resplendent rays of light, his bearing was serious and majestic, his advance measured, his motions composed, his words weighty and powerful, his whole presence displayed a pleasing, kindly gravity and more of godlike qualities than all the other angels until then seen in visible form by the Blessed Virgin Mary. He wore a diadem of exquisite splendor and his vestments glowed in various colors full of refulgent beauty. Encased on his chest, he bore a most beautiful cross, disclosing the mystery of the Incarnation, which He had come to announce. All these circumstances were calculated to rivet the affectionate attention of the Blessed Virgin Mary.

The legions of angels led by holy Gabriel directed their flight to Nazareth, a town of the province of Galilee, to the dwelling place of most holy Mary. This was a humble cottage and her chamber was a narrow room. Mary was at this time fourteen years, six months and seventeen days of age; for her birthday anniversary fell on the eighth of September and six months seventeen days had passed since that date, when this greatest of all mysteries ever performed by God in this world, was enacted in Her.

The bodily shape of the heavenly Queen was well proportioned and taller than is usual with other maidens of her age; yet extremely elegant and perfect in all its parts. Her face was rather more oblong than round, gracious and beautiful, without leanness or grossness; its complexion clear, yet of a slightly brownish hue; her forehead spacious yet symmetrical; her eye brows perfectly arched; her eyes large and serious, of incredible and ineffable beauty and dovelike sweetness, dark in color with a mixture tending toward green; her nose straight and well shaped; her mouth small, with red-colored lips, neither too thin nor too thick.

All the gifts of nature in Her were so symmetrical and beautiful, that no other human being ever had the like. To look upon Her caused feelings at the same time of joy and seriousness, love and reverential fear. She attracted the heart and yet restrained it in sweet reverence; her beauty impelled the tongue to sound her praise, and yet her grandeur and her overwhelming perfections and graces hushed it to silence. In all that approached Her, She caused divine effects not easily explained; She filled the heart with heavenly influences and divine operations, tending toward the Divinity.

Her garments were humble and poor, yet clean, of a dark silvery hue, somewhat like the color of ashes, and they were arranged and worn without pretense, but with the greatest modesty and propriety. At the time when, without her noticing it, legions of angels approached while She was engaged in the highest contemplative prayer concerning the mysteries which God had renewed in Her by so many favors during the nine preceding days. ... the Lord himself had assured Her that His Onlybegotten Son would soon descend to assume human form ... . In those moments, the Archangel Gabriel arrived with his legions of angels. It was on a Thursday at six o clock in the evening and at the approach of night.

The Archangel Gabriel saluted Mary and said: "Ave gratia plena, Dominus tecum, benedictatu in mulieribus!" (Luke 1, 28).
"Hail, full of grace, the Lord is with you, Blessed are you among women!"

"Do not fear, Mary, for thou hast found favor with God; (Luke 1, 30) behold you shall conceive a Son in thy womb, and thou shalt give birth to Him, and you shall name Him Jesus; He shall be great, and He shall be called Son of the Most High." Mary said to Gabriel, what is written by St. Luke: "How shall this happen, that I conceive and bear; since I know not, nor can know, man?" At the same time She interiorly represented to the Lord the vow of chastity, which She had made and the espousal, which His Majesty had celebrated with Her.

The holy prince Gabriel replied (Luke 1, 24): "Mary, it is easy for the Almighty God to make Thee a Mother without the co-operation of man; the Holy Spirit shall remain with Thee by a new presence and the power of the Most High shall overshadow Thee, so that the Holy of Holies can be born of Thee, who shall Himself be called the Son of God. And behold, thy cousin Elisabeth has likewise conceived a son in her sterile years and this is the sixth month of her conception; for nothing is impossible with God. He that can make her conceive, who was sterile, can bring it about, that You, Mary, be His Mother, still preserving thy virginity and enhancing thy purity. To the Son whom You shall bear, God will give the throne of his father David and His reign shall be everlasting in the house of Jacob. Recall my Lady, of the prophecy of Isaias (Is.7, 14), that a Virgin shall conceive and shall bear a son, whose name shall be Emmanuel, God with us. This prophecy is infallible and it shall be fulfilled in You. ..."

With these and many other words, the Archangel Gabriel instructed the most holy Mary, in order that, by the remembrance of the ancient promises and prophecies, by the reliance and trust in them and in the infinite power of the Most High, She might overcome her hesitancy at the heavenly message.

By the intensity of her movements and supernal affections, her most pure heart, as it were by natural consequence, was contracted and compressed with such force, that it distilled three drops of her most pure blood, and these, finding their way to the natural place for the act of conception, were formed by the power of the divine and Holy Spirit, into the body of Jesus Christ our Lord.

Thus the matter, from which the most holy humanity of the Word for our Redemption is composed, was furnished and administered by the most pure heart of Mary and through the sheer force of her true love. At the same moment, with a humility inclining slightly her head and joining her hands, She pronounced these words, which were the beginning of our salvation: "Fiat mihi secundum verbum tuum!" (Luke 1,31). "Let this be done to me according to your word!"

At the pronouncing of this "fiat" so sweet to the hearing of God and so fortunate for us, in one instant, four things happened. First, the most holy body of Jesus Christ our Lord was formed from the three drops of blood furnished by the heart of most holy Mary. Secondly, the most holy soul of the Onlybegotten Son of the Eternal Father was created, just as other souls. Thirdly, the soul and the body united in order to compose His perfect humanity. Fourthly, the Divinity united Itself in the Person of the Word with the humanity, which together became one composite being in hypostatical union; and thus was formed Jesus Christ true God and Man, our Lord and Redeemer. This happened in springtime on the twenty-fifth of March, at the dawning of the day, in the same hour, in which the Creator made Adam.

The divine Child began to grow in the natural manner in the recess of the womb, being nourished by the substance and the blood of His most holy Mother, just as other men. ... Thus in a natural manner the humanity of our Redeemer was nourished, while His Divinity was recreated and pleased with her heroic virtues. Most holy Mary furnished to the Holy Spirit, for the formation of this body, pure and limpid blood, free from sin and all its tendencies. ...

On the day following the Incarnation, the thousand guardian angels which attended to the Blessed Virgin Mary, appeared in corporeal form and with profound humility adored their Incarnate King in the womb of the Blessed Virgin Mary. These angels acknowledged her as their Queen and Mistress and rendered Her due homage and reverence, saying:

"Our Lady, Thou art the true Ark of the testament, since You contain the Lawgiver Himself and preserve the Manna of heaven, which is our true bread. Receive, our Queen, our congratulations on account of thy dignity and happiness, for which we also thank the Most High; since He has fittingly chosen Thee for His Mother and His tabernacle. We offer anew to Thee our homage and service, and wish to obey Thee as vassals and servants of the Supreme and Omnipotent King, whose Mother Thou art." These statements and homages of the holy angels excited in the Mother of God incomparable sentiments of humility, gratitude and love of God. For in her most prudent heart, where all things were weighed with the scales of the sanctuary according to their true value and weight, this reverence and acknowledgment of the angelic spirits proclaiming Her as their Queen, was held in high esteem. Although it was a greater thing to see Herself the Mother of the King and Lord of all creation, yet all her blessings and dignities were made more evident by these demonstrations and homages of the holy angels.

The angels rendered this homage as executors and ministers of the will of the Most High. When their Queen and our Lady was alone, all of them attended to her in physical form, and they assisted Her in her outward actions and tasks; and when she was engaged in manual labor, they administered to her what was needed. Whenever she happened to eat alone in the absence of St. Joseph, they waited upon Her at the poor table and at her humble meals. Everywhere they followed Her and formed an escort, and helped Her in the services performed by St. Joseph. Amid all these favors the Blessed Virgin Mary did not forget to ask permission from God for all her operations and undertakings and to implore His direction and assistance. So exact and so well governed were all her exercises that only God could comprehend and properly weigh them.
Sometimes, in order to afford Her sensible relief, innumerable birds would come to visit Her by the command of the Most High. As if they were endowed with intellect, they would salute Her by their lively movements, and dividing into harmonious choirs, would furnish Her with sweet singing and they would wait for her blessing.

7. Visitation

The Blessed Virgin Mary was informed by the Archangel Gabriel that her cousin Elisabeth (who was thought to be sterile) had conceived a son and that Elisabeth was already in the sixth month of her pregnancy. The Most High revealed to the Blessed Virgin Mary that in a miraculous birth, Elisabeth would bring forth a son, who would be great before God, a Prophet and the Forerunner of the Incarnate Word; also other great mysteries of the holiness and of the personality of St. John were revealed to Her. On this same occasion and on others the Blessed Virgin Mary was informed, that it would be agreeable and pleasing to God, if She would visit her cousin, in order that Elisabeth and her child in her womb might be sanctified by the presence of their Redeemer; for His Majesty was anxious to communicate the benefits of His coming into the world and His merits to His Precursor.

At the news of this sacramental mystery the Blessed Virgin Mary spoke to God and said: "Most High Lord, beginning and cause of all good, let Thy name be eternally glorified, acknowledged and praised by all the nations. I, the least of Thy creatures, give Thee humble thanks for this kindness, which Thou wish to show to Thy servant Elisabeth and to the son of her womb. If it is Your will that I serve Thee in this work, I stand prepared, my Lord, to obey."

The Most High answered Her: "My Dove and my Beloved, elect among creatures, truly I say to thee, that on account of thy intersession and thy love I will, as a Father and generous God, take care of thy cousin Elisabeth and her son, who is to be born to her. I will choose him as my Prophet and as the Precursor of the Word, which is made man in thee; I will look upon them as belonging to thee and intimately connected to thee. Therefore, I wish that My and thy Onlybegotten Son go to see this mother, in order to free her son from the chains of the first sin before the time decreed for other men, his voice and praise may sound up to My ears, and that the mysteries of the Incarnation and Redemption may be revealed to his sanctified soul. Therefore, I wish thee to visit Elisabeth; for We three Persons of the Blessed Trinity have chosen her son for great deeds conformable to Our pleasure."

To this command of God the obedient Blessed Mother responded: "You know, my Lord and God, that all the desires of my heart seek Thy divine pleasure and that I wish to fulfill diligently whatever Thou commands me. Allow me, my God, to ask permission from my husband Joseph and that I make this journey according to his will and direction. And in order that I may not diverge from what is Thy pleasure, do Thou govern me during that journey in all my actions, direct my footsteps to the greater glory of Thy name. Accept therefore the sacrifice, which I bring in going out in public and in leaving my cherished home. I wish to offer more than my desires, my God and King, I hope to be made able to suffer all that will lead to Thy greater service and pleasure purely for Thy love, so that the longings of my soul may not remain entirely unfulfilled."

When the Blessed Virgin Mary came out of this vision, she called upon her thousand angels, who appeared to her in bodily forms, and told them of the command of the Most High. She asked them to assist her carefully in this journey, to teach her how to fulfill all the commands according to the greater pleasure of the Most High, to defend her and guard her from dangers so that she might conduct herself in all things during that journey in the most perfect manner.

With devotion her holy angels offered to obey and serve her. She was herself more wise and more perfect in her deeds than the angels, yet because she was yet in the state of pilgrimage and endowed with a nature lower than that of the angels, she was always anxious to attain perfection by consulting and asking for the help of her guardian angels, though they were her inferiors in sanctity. Under their direction and with the promptings of the Holy Spirit, all her human actions were well ordered. The angels obeyed her quickly as was their ability and due their Queen.

The Blessed Virgin Mary proceeded immediately to ask the consent of St. Joseph for executing the mandate of the Most High, and she said nothing of these happenings, but simply spoke to him these words:

"My lord and spouse, by the divine light it was made known to me, that through condescension of the Most High the prayer of my cousin Elisabeth, the wife of Zacharias, has been heard; she has conceived a son, though she was sterile. Since she has obtained this singular blessing, I hope that through God's infinite bounty, her son will greatly please and glorify the Lord God. I think that on this occasion I am under obligation to visit her and converse with her on certain things for her spiritual encouragement. If this is according to thy liking, I will perform it with thy permission."

St. Joseph answered Mary: "You know already, my Lady and Spouse, that my utmost desires are to serve thee with all diligence and attention; for I am bound to have this confidence in thy great virtue, that you will not do anything, which is not according to the greater pleasure and glory of the Most High; and this is my belief in regard to this journey. ..."

"... Thy making this journey alone and without the company of me thy husband would cause surprise. Therefore, I will gladly go with thee and attend to thy wants on the way. Please appoint the day on which we shall depart together."

The Blessed Virgin Mary thanked St. Joseph for his loving attention and for his cooperation with the will of God in whatever he knew to be for His service and honor. They both concluded to depart immediately on their visit to the house of St. Elisabeth and prepared without delay the provisions, which consisted of a little fruit, bread and a few fish, procured by St. Joseph. In addition to these he borrowed a beast of burden, in order to carry their provisions and the Blessed Mary. And they departed from Nazareth for Juda. "And Mary rising up in those days, went into the hill country with haste, to a city of Juda." (Luke 1, 39).

Leaving the house of her father, Mary and Joseph made their way to the house of Zacharias in mountains of Judea. It was 50 miles from Nazareth, the road was very rough and broken, unfit for a delicate Maiden. She sat on a little donkey for the difficult trip.

Although the humble beast was intended solely for her comfort and service, Mary dismounted many times and asked St. Joseph to ride. He always declined but permitted her now and then to walk with him part of the way. They proceeded alone, without the company of others; but all one thousand angels attended to them. Although the angels accompanied them in physical form they were visible only to Mary.

This journey was the first trip by the Incarnate Word, four days after He had entered the world. During the journey, which lasted four days, they happened upon several very sick people; the Blessed Mother cured all of them and restored them to health.

Mary and Joseph arrived at the city of Juda and at the house of Zacharias. In order to announce their visit, St. Joseph hurried ahead calling out, saying: "The Lord be with you and fill your souls with His divine grace." Elisabeth was already fore warned, for God Himself had informed her in a vision that Mary of Nazareth had departed to visit her.

She had in this vision been made aware that the Blessed Virgin Mary was very pleasing in the eyes of the Most High and informed her that Mary is the Mother of God when they both greeted each other in private. St. Elisabeth immediately came forward with a few of her family to welcome the Blessed Virgin Mary, who was younger. But Mary quickly said: "The Lord be with you, my dearest cousin" and Elisabeth answered: "The same Lord reward you for having come in order to afford me this pleasure." With these words they entered the house of Zacharias.

St. Elisabeth filled with the joy of the Holy Spirit burst forth in a loud voice of praise, pronouncing the words reported by St. Luke: "Blessed are you among women and blessed is the fruit of thy womb. And who am I, that the Mother of my Lord should come to me? As soon as I heard your greeting in my ears, the infant in my womb leaped for joy, and blessed are you, that believed these things shall be accomplished, that were spoken to you by the Lord God."

These words of praise, pronounced by St. Elisabeth were referred by the Blessed Virgin Mary Mother to the Creator; and in the sweetest and softest voice She sang her Magnificat as recorded by St. Luke (Ch. 1, 46-55):

"My soul magnifies the Lord, henceforth generations shall call me blessed. Because He Who is mighty has done great things for me; and Holy is His Name. And His mercy is from generation to generation upon those that fear Him. He has showed might with His arm; He has scattered the proud in their conceit. He has cast down the mighty from their thrones and has raised up the humble. He has filled the hungry with good things; and the rich He has sent away empty. He has received Israel, His servant, being mindful of His mercy; As He spoke to our fathers, to Abraham and his seed forever." Just as St. Elisabeth was the first to hear this sweet canticle from the Blessed Virgin Mary, she was also the first one to understand it.

After staying three days in the house of Zacharias, St. Joseph asked permission of his Spouse Mary to return to Nazareth and leave Her in the company of St. Elisabeth in order to assist in her pregnancy. St. Joseph left with the understanding that he was to return in order to accompany Mary home as soon as they should give him notice. Thus he went on his way back to Nazareth, taking along with him the little donkey which they had brought with them.

The Blessed Virgin Mary stayed with St. Elisabeth for five months. And assisted with the baby (St. John the Baptist) for the last two months.

Returning from the town of Juda to Nazareth the Blessed Virgin Mary traveling on a donkey led by her spouse St. Joseph again took four days in their return journey, as they had done on their coming.

8. The Nativity

i. Joseph notices Mary's pregnancy

The divine pregnancy of the Blessed Virgin Mary had advanced to its fifth month when St. Joseph, her husband, commenced to notice the condition of the Virgin. ... One day, when St. Joseph was full of anxious doubts, and saw Mary coming out of her room, he noticed more particularly her pregnancy. Without doubt, if St. Joseph had believed that Mary had any guilt in causing her pregnancy, he would have died of sorrow. Nobody ever suffered what St. Joseph suffered for sixty days until the Almighty God sent the Archangel Gabriel to him.

All that passed in the heart of St. Joseph was known to the Blessed Virgin Mary, by the light of her divine intelligence. Although her soul was full of tenderness and compassion for the sufferings of her spouse, she said not a word in the matter; but she continued to serve him with all devotion and solicitude.

Full of sadness, which had become intolerable pain, St. Joseph, after saying fervent prayers to the Most High, composed himself for a short sleep, assured that he would wake up at the right time to leave his home at midnight, and, as he thought, without Mary's knowledge. Aware of everything Mary prayed for God to intervene. She knew that the tribulation of her sad spouse had reached a high point, that the time of God's merciful assistance must arrive. The Most High sent His Archangel Gabriel, in order to reveal to St. Joseph during his sleep the mystery of the Incarnation and Redemption in the words recorded in the gospel.

The Archangel spoke to St. Joseph in his sleep, since the mystery was so high, and so difficult to comprehend, especially in his afflicted and troubled state of mind; while this same mystery was made known to others, not while they were asleep, but awake. St. Gabriel said:

39

"Joseph do not be afraid to remain with Mary as her spouse, because what She bears in her womb, is the work of the Holy Spirit. She will give birth to a Son, who shall be called Jesus and He will be the Savior of His people; in all this shall fulfill the prophecy of Isaias, who said (Is. 7, 14): A Virgin shall conceive and shall bring forth a Son, who is to be called Emmanuel, God with us."

St. Joseph did not see the Archangel Gabriel by image, he only heard an interior voice and he understood the mystery. The words of Gabriel imply, that St. Joseph had in his mind already resolved to sever his connection with the Blessed Virgin Mary; for he was told to receive Her again without fear.

St. Joseph awoke with the full consciousness, that his Spouse was the true Mother of God. Full of joy for his good fortune and his inconceivable happiness, and at the same time deeply saddened for what he almost did, he prostrated himself and gave thanks to God for having revealed to him this mystery and for having made him the husband of the Blessed Virgin Mary, whom God had chosen for His Mother, considering that he was not worthy to be even her slave.

During the Blessed Virgin Mary's pregnancy, Lucifer knew She had great power over him. And with seven legions of God's greatest enemies they plotted and mounted an attack on the Blessed Virgin Mary hoping to destroy her. But She prevailed over them as the demons levitated her above the earth, surrounded her and tried to horrify her with great visions of evil. She closed her eyes and ignored them in all of their fury, because she knew the Almighty would not allow them to touch her. After their efforts were frustrated, she was returned to earth and the demons disbanded.

Mary and Joseph lived alone in their house in Nazareth. They had no servants of any kind, not only on account of their humility, but in order more fittingly to hide from any witnesses, the wonders which passed between them which were not to be communicated to outsiders. Mary did not leave her home except in the service of God or her fellow-men.

Never did St. Joseph see the Blessed Mary asleep, nor did he know whether she ever slept, although he asked her to rest, especially during her pregnancy.

The resting place of Mary was the low couch, that had been constructed by St. Joseph; and on it were coverings for her brief sleep.

Her undergarment was a sort of tunic made of cotton, but softer than the ordinary or common cloth. This tunic she never changed from the time since she left the temple, nor did it wear out or grow old or soiled, and no person ever saw it; St. Joseph did not know that she wore that kind of a garment; for he never saw any other part of her clothing except her outside garments, which were open to the view of other persons. Her outer garments were a gray color, and these and her head-coverings were the garments she changed now and then, not because they were soiled, but because, being visible to all, she wished to avoid notice by people. Nothing that She wore became soiled or worn; she never perspired and she was not subjected to other inconveniences or punishments endured by all other human beings. She cared for the clothes and other necessities of St. Joseph. The food of which She ate was limited in kind and quantity. She ate something every day with St. Joseph. She never ate meat, although he did, and she prepared it for him. Her food was fruit, fish, bread and cooked vegetables; she ate in exact measure and weight, only what was necessary for nourishment of the body and to maintain natural warmth without excess.

She acted similarly with her drink. She maintained her eating discipline during her whole life. On occasion Blessed Mary using her God given power, would command the birds of the air to bring some fish from the sea, or fruits of the field, and they would fulfill her commands; sometimes they would bring bread in their beaks, which God had furnished them. St. Joseph was a witness to all these happenings.

They were on some occasions fed by the holy angels. Although St. Joseph labored for others, as did the Blessed Virgin Mary, they never asked for any wages, or set a price on their work, they performed all their work not for gain, but in obedience to a request or for charity, leaving the payment of wages entirely in the hands of their employers and accepting it not as a just payment for their labors, but as a freely given alms. Because of this, often times St. Joseph was not paid for his work.

Therefore, it happened sometimes that they had no food until the Almighty would provide for them. One day their dinner hour passed without anything in the house to eat. They persevered in prayer until very late, giving thanks to God for this privation, and hoping that He would open His all-powerful hand. In the meanwhile, the holy angels prepared the meal and placed upon the table some fruit, bread and fish, also a special preserve or jelly of wonderful sweetness. Then some of the angels went to call their Queen, and others called St. Joseph. Each came forth from their separate resting places and seeing the splendid meal provided by the angels, they thanked the Most High in tears of gratitude and ate the food and afterwards they sang praises to the Almighty.

It had long been the decree of the Most High that the Onlybegotten Son of the Father should be born in the town of Bethlehem (Mich. 5, 2), and accordingly it had been foretold by the Saints and Prophets of from past ages (Jeremiah 10, 9); for the decrees of the absolute will of God are infallible, and nothing can resist them (Esther 13, 9).

To fulfill this immutable decree the Almighty secured by means of an edict of Caesar Augustus for the whole Roman empire, ordering the registration of all the world, as St. Luke says (Luke 2, 1). The Roman empire at that time embraced the greater part of what was then known of the earth and therefore they called themselves masters of the world, ignoring all the other nations. The object of this census was to make all the inhabitants acknowledge themselves as vassals of the emperor, and to pay a certain tax to him.

For this registration everyone had to go to his native city in order to comply. This edict was also proclaimed in Nazareth and St. Joseph heard of it while he was on an errand. He returned to his house and sadly informed the Blessed Virgin Mary of the edict. Where upon, the Blessed Virgin Mary knew the prophecies and that the Messiah would be born in Bethlehem, and consoled St. Joseph.

Then the Almighty gave to the holy guardian angels, in the presence of the Blessed Virgin Mary, a new command that they serve her during this journey with particular care. In addition to the thousand angels which served ordinarily as her guard, the Almighty commanded another nine thousand angels to attend to their Queen and serve as a guard of honor ten thousand strong for her journey. The angels obeyed as the Most High God commanded.

ii. Nazareth to Bethlehem

Mary and Joseph decided on the day of their departure. Joseph diligently searched in the town of Nazareth for some beast of burden to carry the pregnant Blessed Virgin Mary. He could not easily find one because so many people were going to different towns in order to fulfill the requirements of the edict of the emperor. But after searching St. Joseph found an unpretentious little donkey for their journey.

They gathered the articles for a three day journey, which would last five days. Their garments and belongings were the same as that which they had used for their previous journey to the house of Zacharias on their visit to Elisabeth. They took bread, fruit and some fish; their usual food. The Blessed Virgin was enlightened regarding their extended absence and she took linens and clothes necessary for the birth of the Baby Jesus. The Blessed Virgin Mary and St. Joseph departed from Nazareth for Bethlehem alone, poor and humble in the eyes of the world. No one looked upon them with respect because of their poverty and humility.

They did not walk alone, poor or despised, but prosperous, rich and in magnificence; they were most worthy of the immense love of the Eternal Father and most admirable in His eyes. They carried with them the Incarnate Word, the Deity Himself. All of their angelic guard venerated them. They were accompanied by the ten thousand angels, which were appointed by God Himself as the servants of the Blessed Virgin Mary during that whole journey. These legions of angels marched along as their escort in human forms visible to the Blessed Virgin Mary and more brilliant than as many suns.

Their journey lasted five days, because of Mary's pregnancy, St. Joseph shortened each day's journey. Mary and Joseph experienced no darkness of night on the way; when their travel extended beyond nightfall the holy angels emitted their angelic light as if it were day time.

On one of those wintry days they reached a stopping place in the midst of a cold rain and snow storm (for the Almighty did not spare them this inconvenience), and they were obliged to take shelter in stables with animals, because the owners would not furnish better accommodation. The animals showed them the courtesy and kindness which was refused by their fellow human beings. The animals retreated in reverence as their Creator and His Mother, who carried Him in her virginal womb, entered. The Blessed Virgin Mary had command of the winds, the frost and the snow not to inconvenience her; but she would not give the command in order not to deprive herself of suffering in imitation of her Most Holy Son, even before He came into the world. Therefore, the inclemencies of the weather affected Her to a certain extent. St. Joseph did his utmost to shield her as did the holy angels to protect Her, especially the Archangel St. Michael, God's greatest champion, who remained at the right side of his Queen without leaving her for a moment. Several times, when She became tired, St. Michael led her by the arm along the way. Whenever the Most High permitted, God's greatest champion also shielded her against the weather and performed many other services for his Queen and the blessed Fruit of her womb, Jesus.

They arrived at the town of Bethlehem at four o'clock of the fifth day, a Saturday. As it was at the time of the winter solstice, the sun was already sinking and night was falling. They entered the town, and wandered through many streets in search of a lodging, house or inn for staying overnight. They knocked at the doors of their acquaintances and some family relations but they were admitted nowhere and many times they received harsh words and insults. The Blessed Virgin Mary followed St. Joseph through the crowds of people, while he went from house to house and from door to door.

Although She knew that the hearts and the houses of men were to be closed to them, to expose her state of pregnancy at her tender age of fifteen to the public gaze was more painful to her modesty than their failure to procure a lodging. She nevertheless wished to obey St. Joseph and suffer this indignity and unmerited shame. While wandering through the streets they passed the office of the public registry and they wrote their names and paid the tax to comply with the emperor's edict. They continued their search for lodging, having already applied at more than fifty different places, they were rejected and turned away by all of them. The angels were filled with astonishment at the patience and meekness of the powerful but humble Blessed Mary and the uncompassionate hardness of men. At the same time, they blessed the Almighty in all His works and from that day on the Most High began to exalt and honor poverty and humility among men.

It was nine o clock at night when St. Joseph sadly spoke to Mary and said: "My heart is broken with sorrow at not being able to shelter you as you deserve and as I desire, but in not being able to offer you any kind of protection from the weather, or a place of rest. I now remember, that outside the city walls there is a cave, which serves as a shelter for shepherds and their flocks. Let's go there, perhaps it is unoccupied, and we may expect some assistance from God, since we received none from men on earth."

The Blessed Virgin Mary answered: "Joseph, let not your kind heart be afflicted. The cave will be most satisfactory to me. I will be delighted to see you procure it for us." The holy angels accompanied them, brilliantly lighting up the way, and when they arrived at the city gate they saw that the cave was unoccupied, they gave thanks to God.

iii. Jesus is born

The cave which Mary and Joseph chose to occupy was held in such contempt that though the town of Bethlehem was full of strangers in want of shelter, none would demean or degrade themselves to make use of it for a lodging. No one considered it suitable for such a purpose, except Jesus the Savior and His Blessed Mother. On this account the Eternal Father had reserved it for Them.

Blessed Mary and St. Joseph entered the cave provided for them and by the light of the ten thousand angels of their guard they could easily see its poverty and loneliness, which they welcomed with tears of joy. Without delay Mary and Joseph fell on their knees and gave thanks to God. The cave was formed entirely of the bare and coarse rocks, without any natural beauty or artificial adornment; a place intended merely for the shelter of animals; yet the Eternal Father had selected it for the shelter and dwelling place of His Onlybegotten Son.

The angels guarded Blessed Mary their Queen and formed themselves into cohorts in the manner of court guards in a royal palace. They showed themselves in their visible forms also to St. Joseph; for on this occasion it was befitting that he should enjoy such a favor, in order to relieve his sadness by allowing him to see this poor lodging so beautified and adorned by their angelic presence, in order to encourage him for the events which were about to happen during that night in this forsaken place. The Blessed Virgin Mary was already informed of the mystery to be transacted here, set about cleaning with her own hands the cave, which was soon to serve as a royal throne and sacred seat; for neither did she want to miss this occasion for exercising her humility, nor would she deprive her Holy Son of the worship and reverence implied by these preparations.

St. Joseph asked Blessed Mary not to deprive him of this work, which he considered as his alone; and he quickly set about cleaning the floor and the corners of the cave, although she continued to assist him. As the holy angels were present in visible forms, they were astounded at such eagerness for humiliation, and they quickly assisted and filled the cave with holy fragrance. St. Joseph started a fire with the material which he had brought for that purpose. It was very cold, they sat at the fire in order to get warm. They ate the food which they had brought for their frugal supper.

After their supper they gave thanks to God as was their custom. Having spent a short time in this prayer and conferring about the mysteries of the Incarnate Word, holy Mary felt the approach of the most blessed Birth.

She asked St. Joseph to rest and sleep as the night was far advanced. Joseph yielded to her request and asked her to do the same. He arranged and prepared a sort of couch with the articles in their possession, making use of a manger that had been left by the shepherds for their animals. Leaving the Blessed Virgin Mary in the part of the cave he furnished. St. Joseph retired to a corner of the entrance, where he began to pray. He was immediately visited by the Holy Spirit at which he was wrapped and elevated into an ecstasy. In this state St. Joseph was shown all that passed during that night in this holy cave; he would not return to consciousness until the Blessed Virgin Mary called him.

The Blessed Virgin Mary was called from her resting place by a loud voice of the Most High. Immediately, she was filled with new enlightenment and a clear vision of the Divinity. The Most High announced to His Virgin Mother, that the time of His coming into the world had arrived. She prostrated herself before the Throne of His Divinity and gave Him glory, magnificence, thanks and praise for herself and for all creatures, as was befitting of His Divine Love. The Almighty raised her up and gave the Blessed Virgin Mary, her greatest title of *Mother of God*.

He commanded her to exercise this office and ministry as the legitimate and true Mother of Himself; that she should treat Him as the Son of the Eternal Father and at the same time the Son of her body.

The Blessed Virgin Mary remained in this ecstasy of the Beatific Vision for over an hour immediately preceding her divine delivery. At the moment when she came out of the ecstasy and regained the use of her senses she felt and saw that the body of the Infant God move in her womb; releasing and freeing Himself from the place He had occupied for nine months, He prepared to come forth from that sacred chamber. This movement not only did not cause her any pain or hardship, as with all other women but filled her with incomparable joy. At the end of the beatific rapture and vision of the Blessed Virgin Mary was born the Onlybegotten Son of the Eternal Father and of Mary most pure, beautiful and immaculate, leaving her untouched her virginal integrity and purity and making Her more godlike and forever sacred.

The Baby Jesus did not divide, but penetrated the virginal chamber as the rays of the sun penetrate a crystal, lighting it up in prismatic beauty. The Baby Jesus was born pure and disengaged, without the surrounding protective tissue or umbilical cord such as all children are commonly born, and in which they are enveloped in the wombs of their mothers.

God's two greatest champions, the Archangel St. Michael and the Archangel St. Gabriel, were the assistants of the Blessed Mother on this occasion. St. Michael and St. Gabriel stood by at proper distance in human physical forms at the moment when the Incarnate Word, penetrating the virginal chamber by divine power, came forth and the two princes received the Baby Jesus in their hands with extreme reverence. In the same manner as a priest exhibits the sacred host to the people for adoration, so these two Archangels presented to the Blessed Mother her Divine Son. All this happened in a short space of time.

48

Holding the Baby Jesus in her arms she served as the altar and the sanctuary, where the ten thousand angels adored in visible human forms their Creator Incarnate. And as the Most Blessed Trinity assisted in a special manner at the birth of the Word, the Empyrean Heaven was emptied of all its inhabitants, for the whole heavenly court had taken itself to that blessed cave of Bethlehem to adore their Creator in His Mother's arms. In their concert of praise, the holy choirs of angels sang the new canticle: "Gloria in excelsis Deo! et in terra pax hominibus bonae voluntatis." "Glory to God in the highest! And on earth peace and goodwill to men."

It was now time to call St. Joseph from his ecstasy, in which he was informed by divine revelation of all the mysteries of this Sacred Birth during this night. Of all others, St. Joseph had been chosen to act as the guardian and protector of Jesus. The Blessed Virgin Mary intellectually summoned him, he awakened and came forth from his ecstasy. Being restored to consciousness, his first sight was the Baby Jesus in the arms of His Blessed Mother reclining against her breast. St. Joseph adored Jesus in profound humility and with tears of joy. He kissed His feet with great joy and admiration.

St. Joseph handed the Blessed Mother the wrappings and swaddling-clothes, which she had brought. She clothed Him with incomparable reverence, devotion and tenderness. And she laid the Baby Jesus in the manger.

iv. Holy Angels announce the Birth of Jesus

After all of the angels of heaven had celebrated the birth of God made man in the cave of Bethlehem, some of them were immediately sent to different places, in order to announce the joyous news to those who were properly disposed to hear it. The great Archangel St. Michael went to the holy Patriarchs in limbo and announced to them, how the Onlybegotten Son of the Eternal Father was already born into the world and was resting, humble and meek, as they had prophesied, in a manger between two beasts. St. Michael also went in a special manner to holy Joachim and Anne in the name of the Blessed Mother Mary, who had asked him to announce the joyous birth to her parents.

49

St. Michael congratulated Joachim and Anne that their Daughter now held in her arms the Baby Jesus, who had been foretold by all the Patriarchs and Prophets (Is. 7, 14; 9, 7, etc.). It was a most joyful day, for all of these Prophets. St. Joachim and St. Anne asked St. Michael, to ask Mary their Daughter to worship in their name the Divine Baby Jesus. The Blessed Mother did so immediately for her parents, as she listened with great jubilation to the Archangel Michael's report of the joy of the Patriarchs in limbo.

The Blessed Mother sent one of her guardian angels to St. Elisabeth and her son John (St. John the Baptist). Having been informed of what had happened, St. Elisabeth sent a friend to Bethlehem with gifts for the Blessed Mother and the Baby Jesus. The gifts were some money, some linen and other things for the comfort of the Baby Jesus and of His poor Mother and St. Joseph. The friend went directly to visit the Blessed Virgin Mary, the Baby Jesus and St. Joseph, and to bring back certain information of their circumstances. Of the things sent by St. Elisabeth, the Blessed Virgin Mary kept some for relieving their extreme poverty and she distributed the rest of the items to the poor. The Blessed Mother did not wish to be deprived of the company of the poor during the days she would remain in the cave of the Nativity.

Other angels were sent to bring the news to the temple in Jerusalem to Zachary, Simeon and Anne, the prophetess, and to some other holy people, who were worthy to be trusted with this new mystery of our Redemption; for the Lord God found them prepared to receive this news with gratitude and with benefit to themselves, He considered it a just reward for their virtue not to hide from them the blessing conferred upon the human race. Although not all the righteous were informed at that time of this magnificent Gift, all of them were given certain divine effects in the hour in which the Savior of the world was born. For all the just people felt in their hearts a new supernatural joy, though they were ignorant of its cause.

Also there were wonderful movements in the animals; and the stars and planets were renovated and enlivened. The sun became more brilliant; the stars shone in greater brightness; and the Magi Kings were informed of the wonderful star, which showed them the way to Bethlehem (Matt.2,2). Trees began to bloom and others to produce fruit. Some temples of the idols were destroyed; and in others the idols were crushed and their demons hurled into hell. These wonders and other happenings in the world on that day, were explained in different ways by the ignorant.

Many people who by divine inspiration suspected or believed that God had come into the world; yet no one knew it with certainty, except those to whom it was revealed. Among these were the three Magi, to each of whom in their separate Oriental kingdoms, angels of the Blessed Virgin Mary's guard were sent to inform them by intellectual enlightenment that the Redeemer, the Onlybegotten Son of the Eternal Father had been born in poverty and humility. At the same time, they were inspired with the sudden desire of seeking Him and adoring Him and immediately they saw the brilliant star to guide them to Bethlehem.

The shepherds of the region, who were watching their flocks at the time of the birth of Jesus, were especially blessed (Luke 2, 8); not only because they accepted the labor and inconvenience of their calling with resignation from the hand of God, but because, being poor and humble, and despised by the world, they fervently hoped and longed for the coming of the Messiah, speaking and discussing Him among themselves many times. Their attitude resembled that of their God, as they were removed from the riches, vanity and ostentation of the world and far from its diabolical cunning. They acted in the circumstances of their position similar to the Good Shepherd that had come to know His Sheep and being known by them. The shepherds were invited as the first fruits of the saints by the Savior Himself, to be the very first ones, to whom the Eternal Incarnate Word manifested Himself and by whom He wished to be praised, served and adored.

51

The Archangel Gabriel was sent to them as they watched on the field, appearing to them in human form and in great splendor. The shepherds were suddenly enveloped in the celestial radiance of the mighty Archangel, and at his sight they were filled with great fear.

St. Gabriel reassured them and said: "Ye upright men, be not afraid: for I announce to you tidings of great joy, which is for you, today is born the Redeemer Christ, our Lord God in the city of David. And as a sign of this truth, I tell to you, that you shall find the Infant wrapped in swaddling-clothes and lying in a manger." (Luke 2, 10, 12).

At these words of the Archangel Gabriel there suddenly appeared a great multitude of angel choirs, who in harmony sang to the Most High these words: "Glory to God in the highest and on earth peace to men of goodwill." Repeating this divine phrase, the holy angels disappeared. All this happened in the fourth watch of the night (just before daylight). By this magnificent angelic vision, the humble and fortunate shepherds were enlightened and hurried to see with their own eyes the divine mystery of which they had been informed. The signs which the holy angels had indicated to the shepherds did not seem appropriate or proportioned for attesting the greatness of the Newborn to eyes of the flesh. For to lie in a manger and to be wrapped in swaddling-clothes, would not have been convincing proof of the majesty of a king, if these shepherds had not been enlightened by the Most High God and been enabled to penetrate the mystery.

As they were free from the arrogant wisdom of the world, they were easily made to believe. Discussing this message, they resolved to hurry to Bethlehem and see the wonder made known to them by the Lord God.

They departed without delay and entering the cave, they found, as St. Luke tells us, Mary and Joseph, and the Infant lying in a manger. Seeing all this, the shepherds recognized the truth of what they had heard of the Child. When the shepherds looked upon the Baby,

He looked at them, emitting from His Face great radiance that wounded them with love and changed them and renewed them in a new state of grace and holiness and filling them with an exalted knowledge of the divine mysteries of the Incarnation and the Redemption of the human race.

Prostrating themselves on the earth they adored the Word made flesh. Not any more as ignorant impoverished shepherds but as wise and prudent men they adored Him, acknowledged and magnified Him as true God and man, as Restorer and Redeemer of the human race. The Blessed Mother took notice of all that they did interiorly and exteriorly; for she saw into their inmost hearts. She preserved the memory of all these happenings and pondered them in her soul, with the other mysteries and with the holy prophecies and sayings of the Scriptures. She spoke to the shepherds, instructing them to persevere in the service of the Most High. They conversed with the Blessed Virgin Mary and showed her by their answers that they understood many of the mysteries. They remained in the cave from the beginning of dawn until mid-day. After she gave them something to eat, she sent them away full of heavenly grace. During the days when the Blessed Mother, the Child and St. Joseph remained in the cave of Bethlehem, these holy shepherds returned a few times and brought gifts as their poverty could spare. The shepherds were unable to spread the news until after the Blessed Mother, the Child and St. Joseph had departed and fled from the neighborhood of Bethlehem. Not all of those that heard the shepherds speaking about the Holy Infant believed them, for they held them in contempt as uncultured and ignorant people. However, these shepherds were saints filled with divine knowledge until they died.

Among those who believed them was Herod, but not because of any laudable faith or piety, but on account of his worldly and wicked fear of losing his kingdom.

Among the children, who would be martyred by him, there were some belonging to these holy shepherds. Their parents consented joyfully to the martyrdom, which the children themselves desired and offering themselves up to the Lord God, whom they were made to know, beforehand.

Lucifer and his demons were left in ignorance of many things, which they could naturally have known concerning the Incarnation of the Word and other events in the course of His most holy life, a fact which it is necessary to take notice of in this history. But if Lucifer had known for certain, that Jesus was the true God, he would not have procured His death, but he would have sought to prevent it. Concerning the mystery of the Nativity, Lucifer only knew that the Blessed Virgin Mary had given birth to a Son in poverty and in a forsaken cave, and that she had not found even lodging and shelter; that the Child was circumcised and otherwise treated as mere man; all of which would mislead him in his pride rather than to enlighten him. For the wits of Lucifer are no match for the Omnipotent Most High God. Lucifer was ignorant of the manner of Birth of the Incarnate Word and of the virginity of the Blessed Mother before and after the Birth. Also Lucifer was ignorant of the message of the angels to God's chosen, as well as to the shepherds and their conversations and of their adoration of the Infant God. Lucifer and his demons did not see the brilliant star, nor did he know the purpose of the Magi Kings coming to Bethlehem, although he saw them make the journey and attributed it to some worldly enterprise. The demons were also unable to account for the changes in the elements, the stars and planets; though they saw these changes and wonderful effects. They misjudged the words of the Magi in the presence of Herod, their arrival at the stable and the adoration, and the gifts offered.

The demons saw the fury of Herod against the children and encouraged it; yet they did not understand his objective and they stirred up his cruelty.

Although Lucifer suspected that Herod was seeking to kill the Messiah, he considered him demented and treated him with disdain. For in his pride Lucifer obstinately held fast to the opinion, that the Word, upon entering into the world in order to establish His Kingdom, would therefore not come humbly and in a hidden manner, but with ostentatious power and majesty, while in reality the Infant God chose a far different way, being born of a Mother poor and despised by men.

Thus misled, Lucifer, having noticed some of the strange events connected with the Nativity, called together his demons in hell, and said to them: "I do not find any occasion for fear in the events, which we have noticed in the world. It is true, the Woman whom we persecuted so much, has given birth to a Son, but in such poverty and neglect, that She could not even procure a lodging-place in order to be delivered. We know all this to be far from the power and greatness of the Most High God. If God is to take advantage over us by this weak vulnerable Child as we have assured ourselves concerning Him then He certainly cannot take advantage against our power. We need not fear that this Child is the Messiah, since there is even a plot to kill Him as being mortal like the rest of men. This does not seem to point to the salvation of the world, since He Himself seems to stand in need of atoning for His fault by death. All these signs conflict with the purpose of the Messiah in coming into the world and therefore it seems to me, that we can rest assured, that the Messiah has not yet come."

The demons approved of the decision of their damned chief and they were all satisfied, that the Messiah had not yet come, for they were all accomplices in the malice and pride which blinded Lucifer. It never occurred to Lucifer in his vanity and indomitable pride, that the majesty and greatness of God should humiliate itself; because he himself sought after applause, ostentation, reverence and exaltation, wishing if possible to appropriate all honor to himself. Since all honor was attainable by God, it never entered Lucifer's mind, that God would consent to the contrary and subject Himself to humiliation, so much abhorred by evil spirits.

All these errors and insanities of Lucifer and his demons were known to the Blessed Mother our Queen and with a just appreciation of such high mysteries she magnified and blessed the Most High God, because He had concealed His magnificent plans from the proud and arrogant and revealed them to the poor and humble. The Blessed Mother offered up fervent prayers for all of humanity, who because of their faults were unworthy of seeing the Light and she reminded her most Holy Son to have compassion and love for sinners. In these prayers she spent most of the time in the cave of the Nativity.

But as this place was bare of all comfort and much exposed to inclemencies of weather, the Blessed Mother was most cautious for the shelter of her tender and Holy Child. As a most prudent Mother she had brought a mantle, with which she covered Him in addition to the ordinary swaddling-clothes. She held Jesus continually in the embrace of her arms, except when to make St. Joseph happy, she asked him to hold the Incarnate God in his arms and serve him as a father.

The first time she placed the Infant God in St. Joseph's arms, the Blessed Mother said to him: "My husband and my helper, receive in thy arms the Creator of heaven and earth and enjoy His amiable and sweet company, in order that my Lord and my God may be delighted by thy faithful services. Take to thyself the Treasure of the Eternal Father and participate in this blessing of the human race."

9. Jesus is Circumcised

The Most High spoke to the Blessed Virgin Mary saying: "My Daughter and my Dove, do not let thy heart be afflicted because thy Son is to be subjected to the knife and to the pains of circumcision. I have sent Him into the world as an example, that He put an end to the law of Moses by entirely fulfilling it. Though it is true that the habitation of His humanity, which thou hast given Him as his natural Mother, is to be violated, and his flesh wounded together with thy soul, yet remember: He is my natural Son by an eternal generation the image of my substance, equal to Me in essence, majesty and glory, and subjects Himself to the sacramental law and freedom from sin without letting man know that He is exempt from sin as He suffers for man. Thou knows beforehand, my Daughter, that thou must reserve thy Son and my Onlybegotten for this and other greater sufferings. Resign thyself, then, to the shedding of His blood and willingly yield to Me the first fruits of the eternal salvation of men."

To this decree of the Eternal Father the Blessed Virgin Mary, as the Co-redempterist of our salvation, conformed herself. In most loving obedience she offered up her Son, saying: "Supreme Lord and God, I offer to Thee this Victim and Host of acceptable sacrifice with all my heart, although I am full of compassion and sorrow that men have offended Your immense Goodness in such a way as to force a God to make amends. Eternally shall I praise Thee for looking with such infinite love upon Thy creatures and for preferring to refuse pardon to Thy own Son rather than hinder the salvation of man. I, who by Thy selection am His Mother, must before all other mortals subject myself to Thy pleasure and therefore I offer to Thee the most meek Lamb, which is to take away the sins of the world by His innocence."

The Blessed Virgin Mary arose from her prayer and asked St. Joseph to take the necessary steps for the Circumcision of the Divine Infant. She did not tell him anything of what she had been told by the Most High.

She spoke as if she wished to consult him or ask his opinion in regard to the Circumcision, saying that the time appointed by law for the Circumcision of the Child had arrived and since they had not received any orders to the contrary, it seemed necessary to comply with it.

They themselves, she said, were more bound to please the Most High, to obey more punctually his precepts, and to be more zealous in the love and care of His Most Holy Son than all the rest of creatures, seeking to fulfill in all things the Divine pleasure in return for His incomparable favors. St. Joseph answered as no command to the contrary had been given concerning the Child, he wished in all things to conform himself to the divine will manifested in the common law; although as God the Incarnate Word was not subject to the law, yet He was now clothed with our humanity, and, as a most perfect Teacher and Savior, no doubt wished to conform with other men in its fulfillment. Then he asked the Blessed Mother how the Circumcision was to take place.

The Blessed Virgin Mary answered, that the Circumcision should be performed substantially in the same way as it was performed on other children; but that she would not hand Him over or consign Him to any other person, but that she would herself hold Him in her arms, as He was circumcised. And because of His awareness and tenderness this ritual would be more painful to Him than to other children, they should have soothing medicine, which was ordinarily applied at circumcision. She requested St. Joseph to procure a crystal or glass vessel for preserving the sacred relic of the Circumcision of the Divine Infant.

The cautious Mother prepared some linen cloth to catch the sacred blood, which was now for the first time to be shed for our salvation so that not one drop of His blood would be lost or fall upon the ground. After these preparations the Blessed Mother asked St. Joseph to inform the priest and request him to come to the cave so it would not be necessary to take the Child to any other place. That he might, as a fit and worthy minister of so hidden and great a sacrament, with his priestly hands perform the rite of the Circumcision in the cave.

The Blessed Virgin Mary and St. Joseph discussed the name to be given to the Divine Infant in the Circumcision, and St. Joseph said: "My Lady, when the holy Archangel of the Most High informed me of this great sacrament, he also told me that thy most sacred Son should be called JESUS." The Blessed Mother answered: "This same name was revealed to me when He assumed flesh in my womb; and thus receiving this name from the Most High through the mouth of His holy angels and ministers, it is fitting that we obey His inscrutable judgments of His infinite wisdom in conferring it on my Son and Lord, and that we call Him JESUS. This name we will propose to the priest, for inscription in the register with the names of the other circumcised children.

While the Blessed Virgin Mary and St. Joseph conversed with each other, multitudes of angels descended in human forms from the Empyrean Heaven clothed in shining white garments, on which were woven red embroideries of wonderful beauty. They had palms in their hands and crowns upon their heads emitted a greater brilliance than many suns. In comparison with the beauty of these holy angels the beauty seen in the world appeared repulsive. On the chest of each angel the holy name of 'Jesus' was engraved or embossed. The brilliance and radiance that these emblems emitted exceeded that of all the angels together, and the variety of the beauty displayed by this great multitude was so exquisite, no words can describe. The holy angels divided into two choirs in the cave, keeping their gaze fixed upon their King and God in the arms of His Blessed Mother. The leaders of these heavenly choirs were the great Archangels St. Michael and St. Gabriel, shining in greater splendor than the rest and bearing in their hands, the most holy name of JESUS, written in larger letters on something like cards of incomparable beauty and splendor.

The two Archangels presented themselves apart from the rest before their Queen and said: "Our Lady, this is the name of thy Son, which was written in the mind of God from all eternity and which the Blessed Trinity has given to His Onlybegotten Son and our Lord as a sign of salvation for the whole human race; establishing Him on the throne of David.

He shall reign upon it, chastise His enemies and triumph over them, making them His footstool and passing judgment upon them; He shall raise His friends to the glory of His right hand. But all this is to happen at the cost of suffering and blood; and even now He is to shed it in receiving this name, since it is that of the Savior and Redeemer; it shall be the beginning of His sufferings in obedience to the will of His Eternal Father. We have all come as ministering spirits of the Most High, appointed and sent by the Holy Trinity in order to serve the Onlybegotten Son of the Father and thy own Son in all the mysteries and sacraments of the law of grace. We are to accompany Him and minister to Him until He shall ascend triumphantly to the Empyrean Heaven and open the gates of heaven; afterwards we shall enjoy a special glory beyond that of the other blessed, to whom no such commission has been given."

All this was witnessed by St. Joseph together with the Blessed Virgin Mary; but his understanding of these happenings was not so deep as hers, for the Mother of God understood and comprehended the highest mysteries of the Redemption. The Blessed Virgin Mary sent St. Joseph to Bethlehem to bring the priest to the cave. The priest came to the cave of the Nativity, where the Incarnate Word was resting in the arms of His Blessed Mother. ... The priest permitted the Child to be held in the arms of His Mother.

The Blessed Mother then unwound the swaddling clothes in which her most Holy Son was wrapped and drew from her bosom a linen cloth, which she had previously placed there for the purpose of warming it; for the weather was very cold on that day. While holding the Child in her hands she placed a linen cloth that the relics and the blood of the Circumcision would fall upon it. The priest proceeded to circumcise the Holy Child and asked the parents what name they wished to give to the Child in Circumcision. Mary and Joseph said at the same time: "JESUS is His name." The priest answered: "The parents are agreed, and great is the name which they give to the Child." He wrote Jesus in the tablet or register with the names of the other children. While writing it the priest said: "I am convinced that this Child is to be a great Prophet of the Lord. Take great care in raising Him, ..."

60

10. Magi Kings come with gifts for the Baby Jesus

By her knowledge of Holy Scriptures and her supernatural enlightenment, the Blessed Virgin Mary knew that the Magi Kings from the east would come to acknowledge and adore her most holy Son as their true God. She was aware of it because an angel had been sent to them to announce the birth of the Incarnate Word and the Blessed Mother was not ignorant of this message. St. Joseph had no knowledge of these mysteries because they had not been revealed to him, nor had the Blessed Mother informed him of this secret. After the Circumcision, St. Joseph suggested to the Blessed Mother that they leave their poor and forsaken cave because it was an inadequate shelter for the Divine Infant and for her and it would now be possible to find lodging in Bethlehem, where they could remain until after presenting the Child in the temple of Jerusalem. This proposal of St. Joseph arose from his anxiety that the Child and Mother should want comfort and convenience which they could afford. He left it all to the Blessed Virgin Mary's discretion. She made use of her God given power whenever the rigors of winter rose to excess. She would command the frost and the winds, the snow and the ice not to inflict their Creator, and to spend their elemental fury and asperity upon her person alone.

The elements obeyed the Mother of God: for upon her command, the snow and rain approached no nearer than ten yards, the winds stopped short and the surrounding air retained a mild temperature. To this miracle was added another one, at the same time in which the Divine Infant in her arms received this homage by the elements and was protected from their fury, the Blessed Mother felt and suffered the cold and inclemency of the weather as if it were exerting all its natural influences on her.

In this they obeyed the Loving Mother and sovereign Mistress of creatures to the letter, as she wished not to exempt herself from their harshness while she prevented her tender Child and her God from suffering under it. St. Joseph enjoyed the same privilege as the Holy Infant. St. Joseph noticed the favorable change of the temperature, without knowing that it was due to the commands of the Blessed Mother.

The Blessed Mother offered Jesus her breast milk three times a day, and always with such reverence that she asked His permission beforehand and His pardon for the indignity. Jesus returned His Mother's caresses by His facial expressions of pleasure and by other actions typical of children. The most ordinary token of His love was to recline upon the breast of His Blessed Mother, or upon her shoulder, encircling her neck with His arms.The three Magi Kings, who came to find the Divine Infant after His birth in the cave of Bethlehem, were natives of Persia, Arabia and Sabba (Ps. 71, 10), countries to the east of Israel. Their coming was prophesied especially by David.

The three Kings were well versed in the natural sciences, and well read in the Scriptures of the Jews; and because of their extensive learning they were called Magi. By their knowledge of Scripture, and by conferring with some of the Jews, they believed in the coming of the Messiah expected by Jews. They were upright men, truthful and very just in the governing of their countries. Since their kingdoms were relatively small, they governed them easily, and personally administered justice as wise and prudent sovereigns.

Because these Magi governed adjoining countries and lived not far from each other, they were mutual friends and shared with each other the virtues and the knowledge which they had acquired, consulting each other in the more important events of their reigns. In all things they communicated with each other as most faithful friends.

It happened in the following manner: one of the guardian angels of the Blessed Virgin Mary of a higher order than that of the guardian angels of the three kings, was sent from the cave of the Nativity. By his superior faculties he enlightened the three guardian angels of the Kings informing them at the same time of the will and command of the Most High God that each of them should manifest to his charge the mystery of the Incarnation and of the birth of Christ our Redeemer. Immediately and in the same hour each of the three angels spoke in dreams to the wise man under his care. This is the usual course of angelic revelations when the Lord communicates with souls through the angels.

This enlightenment of the Magi Kings concerning the mysteries of the Incarnation was very extensive and clear. They were informed that the King of the Jews was born as true God and man, that He was the Messiah and Savior who was expected; that it was the One who was promised in the Scriptures and prophecies (Gen. 3, 10) ; and that they themselves, the three Kings, were chosen by God to seek the star. Each one of the three Kings also was made aware that the same revelation was being made to the other two in the same way; and that this knowledge was to be used, and they were expected to follow the star to its resting place. They were inspired and inflamed with a great love and with a desire to know the God made man, to adore Him as their Creator and Redeemer, and serve Him with perfect devotion. In all this they were greatly assisted by their moral virtues, which they had acquired and were excellently disposed for this divine enlightenment.

After receiving these heavenly revelations in their sleep, the three Kings awoke at the same hour of the night, and prostrating themselves on the ground and humiliating themselves to the dust, they adored in spirit the immense being of God. They praised His infinite mercy and goodness for having sent the Divine Word to assume flesh of a Virgin (Is. 7, 14) in order to redeem the world and give eternal salvation to men. Then all three of them, governed by an impulse of the Holy Spirit, resolved to depart without delay for Judea in search of the Divine Child in order to adore Him. The three Kings prepared gifts of gold, incense and myrrh in equal quantities, being guided by the same mysterious impulse; and without having conferred with each other concerning their undertaking, the three of them arrived at the same resolve and the same plan. In order to set out immediately, they procured on the same day the necessary camels and provisions together with a number of servants for the journey. Without heeding the commotion caused among their people, or considering that they were to travel in foreign regions, or caring for any outward show of authority, without ascertaining particulars of the place where they were to go, or gathering information for identifying the Child, they immediately departed in order to find the newborn King.

63

At the same time the great holy angel, who had brought the news from Bethlehem to the kings, formed of the material air a most resplendent star, although not so large as those of the firmament; for it was not to ascend higher than was necessary for the purpose of its formation. It took its course through the atmospheric regions in order to guide and direct the holy Kings to the cave, where the Child awaited them. Its splendor was of a different kind from that of the sun and the other stars; with its most beautiful light it illumined the night like a brilliant torch, and despite the sun the Star of Bethlehem by its brilliance could be seen by day.

On coming out of their palaces each one of the kings saw this new star (Matt. 2, 2) although each from a different standpoint, because it was only one star and it was placed in such distance and height that it could be seen by each one at the same time.

As the three of them followed the guidance of this miraculous star, they soon met. Thereupon it immediately approached them more closely, descending through many shifts of the aerial space and rejoicing them by shining its brilliance over them at closer range. They began to discuss among themselves about the revelation they had received and about their plans, finding that they were identical. They were more and more inflamed with devotion and with the pious desire of adoring the newborn God, and broke out in praise and admiration at the magnificent works and mysteries of the Almighty.

The Magi followed their journey under the guidance of the star without losing sight of it until they arrived at Jerusalem. They suspected that this was the birthplace of their legitimate and true King, because Jerusalem was the capital of Israel. They entered into the city and openly inquired about Him, saying (Matt. 2, 8). "Where is the king of the Jews, who is born? For we have seen his star in the East, announcing to us His Birth and we have come to see Him and adore Him." Their inquiry came to Herod, who at that time unjustly reigned in Judea and lived in Jerusalem.

The wicked king, panic-stricken at the thought that a more legitimate claimant to the throne should have been born, was very disturbed and outraged by this report. With him the whole city was aroused, some of the people, out of flattery to the king, others on account of the fear of disturbance. Immediately, as St. Matthew relates, Herod called together a meeting of the principal priests and scribes in order to ask them where Christ was to be born according to the prophecies and holy Scriptures.

They answered that, according to the words of one of the Prophets, Micheas (Mich. 5, 2), He was to be born in Bethlehem; since it was written by him that thence the Ruler of Israel was to arise.

Thus informed of the birthplace of the new King of Israel, and insidiously plotting from that very moment to destroy Him, Herod dismissed the priests. Then he secretly called the Magi in order to learn from them at what time they had seen the star announcing His Birth (Matt. 2, 7). They ingenuously informed him, and he sent them away to Bethlehem, saying to them in covert malice: "Go and inquire about the Infant, and when you have found Him, tell me, in order that I, too, may go to recognize and adore Him." The Magi departed, leaving the hypocritical king ill at ease and in great consternation at such indisputable signs of the coming of the legitimate King of Israel into the world. Although he could have eased his mind in regard to His sovereignty by the thought that a recently born infant could not be enthroned so very soon, yet human prosperity is so unstable and deceitful that it can be over thrown even by an infant, or by the mere threat of far-off danger. Thus can imagined uncertainty destroy all the enjoyment and happiness so deceitfully offered to its possessors.

On leaving Jerusalem the Magi saw the star again, which at their entrance into Jerusalem had disappeared from their view. By its light they were guided to Bethlehem and to the cave of the Nativity. Diminishing in size it hovered over the Head of the Infant Jesus and bathed Him in its light; then at that moment the matter of which the star had been composed dissolved and disappeared.

The Blessed Virgin Mary had already been prepared by the Most High for the coming of the Kings, and when she understood that they were approaching the cave, she requested St. Joseph not to leave it, but to stay at her side.

The Magi had been instructed that the Mother of the Newborn God was a Virgin, and that He was the true God and not a son of St. Joseph. Nor would God have permitted them to be led to the cave ignorant of such an important fact as His origin, allowing them to adore the Child as the son of Joseph and of a Mother not a Virgin. They were fully instructed as to all these mysteries, and they were deeply impressed. The heavenly Mother awaited the pious and devout kings, standing with the Holy Child in her arms. Amid the humble and poor surroundings of the cave, in incomparable modesty and beauty, she exhibited at the same time a majesty more than human, the light of heaven shining in her countenance. Still more visible was this light in the Child, resplendent throughout the cave which made it like a heaven. The three kings of the East entered and at the first sight of the Son and Mother they were for a considerable space of time overwhelmed with wonder. They prostrated themselves upon the earth, and in this position they worshiped and adored the Infant, acknowledging Him as the true God and man, and as the Savior of the human race. By the divine power, which the sight of Him and His presence exerted in their souls, they were filled with new enlightenment. They saw the multitude of angels who as servants and ministers of the King of kings and Lord of lords attended upon Him with reverential fear (Heb. 1, 4). Arising, they congratulated their Queen, the Blessed Virgin Mary as Mother of the Son of the Eternal Father; and they approached to reverence Her on their knees. They sought her hand in order to kiss it, as they were accustomed to do to queens in their countries. But the most prudent Blessed Mother withdrew her hand, and offered instead the Hand of the Baby Jesus saying: "My spirit rejoices in the Lord and my soul blesses and extols Him; because among all the nations He has called and selected you to look upon and behold that which many kings and prophets have in vain desired to see, namely, Him who is the Eternal Word Incarnate (Luke 10, 24). Let us honor and praise His name because of the great mysteries given to His people; let us kiss the earth which He sanctifies by His real presence."

At these words of the Blessed Virgin Mary, the three kings humbled themselves adoring the Infant Jesus; they acknowledged the great blessings of living in the time when the Onlybegotten Son of the Eternal Father was arising in order to illumine the darkness (Malachy 4, 2). Thereupon they spoke to St. Joseph, congratulating him for his good fortune in being chosen as the spouse of the Mother of God; and they expressed wonder and compassion at the great poverty, beneath which were hidden the greatest mysteries of heaven and earth. Their discussion lasted three hours, and then the kings asked permission of most holy Mary to go to the city in order to seek a lodging, as there was no room for them in the cave. Some people had accompanied them; but the Magi alone participated in the light and the grace of this visit. The others took notice merely of what passed exteriorly, and witnessed only the destitute and neglected condition of the Holy Family. Though in wonder at the strange event, they perceived nothing of its mystery. The Magi departed and left Mary and Joseph alone with their Child. The Magi glorified His Majesty with new songs of praise, because His name was beginning to be known and adored among the Gentiles.

During these blessed conversations the Magi remembered the dire destitution of Jesus, Mary and Joseph in their cave, and they resolved immediately to send them some gifts in order to show their affection and to satisfy their desire of serving them, since they could not do anything else for them. They sent through their servants many of the gifts, which they had brought for the Holy Family. The Blessed Virgin Mary and St. Joseph received these gifts with humble thanks and in gratitude returned to them many powerful blessings for the spiritual comfort of the three Kings. The Kings went to rest full of incomparable joy in the Lord God; and in their sleep the angels advised them as to their journey homeward.

On the following day at dawn they returned to the cave of the Nativity in order to offer to the heavenly King the special gifts which they had brought. Arriving they prostrated themselves anew in profound humility; and opening their treasures, as Scripture relates, they offered Him gold, incense and myrrh (Matt. 2, 11).

They consulted the Blessed Mother in regard to many mysteries and practices of faith, and concerning matters pertaining to their consciences and to the governing of their countries; for they wished to return well instructed and capable of directing themselves in justice, holiness and perfection in their daily life. As a Teacher and an instrument of divine wisdom she answered all their questions, giving them such great knowledge that they did not want to leave. However, an angel of God appeared to them, reminding them of the necessity and of the Will of the Almighty that they should return to their country.

The heavenly Mother received the gifts of the Kings and in their name offered them to the Infant Jesus. His Majesty showed by signs of highest pleasure, that He accepted their gifts: they themselves became aware of the exalted and heavenly blessings with which He repaid them more than a hundredfold (Matt. 19, 29). According to the custom of their country they also offered to Mary the Queen of Heaven some gems of great value; but because these gifts had no mysterious signification and did not refer to Jesus, she returned them to the Kings. She received only the gifts of gold, incense and myrrh. In order to send them home more joyful, she gave them some of the clothes in which she had wrapped the Infant God; for she had no greater visible gifts of higher honor with which to give them at their departure. The three Kings received these relics with such reverence and esteem that they encased them in gold and precious stones in order to keep them ever after. As a proof of their value these relics emitted a unique fragrance that they revealed their presence to those around. However, only those who believed in the coming of God into the world were able to smell it; while nonbelievers could not smell anything emitted by the relics. In their own countries the Magi performed great miracles with these relics.

The holy Kings also offered their property and possessions to the Blessed Mother and to Jesus. But if she did not wish to accept them and preferred to live in this place, where her most Holy Son had been born, they would build her a house, where they could live more comfortably. The Blessed Mother thanked them for their offers without accepting them. The three Kings asked her and St. Joseph not to forget them.

With the blessing of Jesus, Mary and Joseph, the three Kings departed. They chose another way for their return journey, in order not to meet Herod in Jerusalem; as they had been instructed by the angel the prior night. On their departure from Bethlehem a similar star appeared in order to guide them home, conducting them on their new route to the place where they had first met. There they each separated to return to his own country.

For the rest of their lives these three Kings lived up to their divine enlightenment governing both their souls and the people of their countries according to the Blessed Virgin Mary's teaching.

To summarize the gifts of the three Magi Kings were identical by divine inspiration, each King brought three chests of equal size each with the same contents of gold, incense and myrrh. Therefore, together they brought three equal chests filled with gold, three filled with incense, and three filled with myrrh. According to the Blessed Virgin Mary, there was a great amount of gold; enough gold that the Holy Family could have lived in luxury their entire lives. The Blessed Mother would not ever touch money but would ask St. Joseph to handle all circumstances involving money. She commanded that all of the incense and myrrh be sold and the money obtained be distributed amongst the poor. St. Joseph kept a small amount of the gold. Most of the gold was also given to the poor. St. Joseph would use the little amount of gold he kept for two purposes: first, to purchase a tiny house in Egypt; second, to purchase a small plot of ground next to their home in Nazareth upon their return from Egypt. The Holy Family would use this small plot of ground to grow fruits and vegetables for their food.

11. The Presentation of Jesus in the Temple

After the departure of the three Kings and after the due celebration of the great mystery of the adoration of the Infant Jesus, there was really nothing to wait for in that poor yet sacred place, and they were free to leave it. The most prudent Mother then said to St. Joseph: "My master and spouse, the offerings which the Kings have made to our God and Child must not remain here idle; but they must be applied in the service of His Majesty and should be used according to His will and pleasure. I deserve nothing, even of temporal goods; dispose of all these gifts as belonging to my Son and to thee."

St. Joseph answered, with his accustomed humility and courtesy, that he would leave all to Her and would be pleased to see Her dispose of them. But Mary insisted and said: "... dispose of them for love of the poor, who are waiting for their share; they have a right to the things which their heavenly Father has created for their sustenance." They therefore immediately concluded to divide the gifts into three parts: one destined for the temple of Jerusalem, namely the incense and myrrh, as well as part of the gold; another part as offering to the priest, who had circumcised the Child, in order that he might use it for himself and for the synagogue in Bethlehem, and the third part for distribution among the poor. This resolve they executed with generous and fervent affection.

The Almighty made use of a poor but honorable and pious woman to be the reason for their leaving the cave. In order to relieve her poverty the Blessed Virgin Mary gave her some of the gold destined for the poor. Thereby the condition of this fortunate woman was much improved and she invited the Holy Family to live in her poor house.

Mary and Joseph discussed the invitation and agreed to leave the cave and lodge in the house of this woman; and stay there until the time of the purification and the presentation in the temple. They did it willingly as it allowed them to remain near the cave of the Nativity; and because many people began to frequent the cave because of the rumor of the visit of the Kings, which had been spread.

70

The Holy Family accepted the hospitality of the kind woman, who received them with the greatest charity and assigned to them the larger portion of her dwelling. The holy angels and ministers of the Most High accompanied them in human forms, which they had always retained. When the Baby Jesus and His Blessed Mother left the cave, God appointed an angel as its keeper and watcher, as He had done with the garden of Paradise (Gen. 3, 24). And this guard remained and does remain to this day sword in hand at the opening of the cave; and stands guard to protect the sacred cave from desecration or destruction.

The Holy Family remained in the kind woman's house until the time for the Presentation in the Temple of Jerusalem. Forty days after the birth of Jesus according to the law, a woman was to go to the temple to be purified and all first born sons were to be presented to God in the Temple.

On the following morning, the Holy Family proceeded to the Temple in Jerusalem two hours away. The ten thousand angels and a great multitude of other angels descended from the Empyrean Heaven with shields bearing the Holy Name of Jesus. Only Jesus and His Blessed Mother could see the additional angels.

When they arrived at the temple-gate, the Blessed Mother was immersed in an intellectual vision of the Blessed Trinity and she heard a voice issuing from the Eternal Father, saying: "This is my beloved Son, in whom I am well pleased." (Matt. 27, 20). St. Joseph felt at the same time the Holy Spirit, which filled him with joy. The holy high-priest Simeon, moved by the Holy Spirit, entered the temple at the same time. He approached the Blessed Virgin Mary holding the Infant Jesus in her arms. The prophetess Anne, had come at the same hour, and she and Simeon saw Mary and Jesus surrounded by a wonderful light. In their spirit of joy, Simeon and Anne approached them; and the priest received the Infant Jesus from her arms upon his hands.

71

Raising up his eyes to heaven he offered Him up to the eternal Father, pronouncing at the same time these words so full of mysteries: "Now dost thou dismiss thy servant, O Lord, according to thy Word in peace. Because my eyes have seen thy salvation, which thou hast prepared before the face of all peoples; a light for the revelation of the gentiles, and the glory of thy people Israel." (Luke 2, 29). Then Simeon speaking to the Blessed Mother said: "Behold this Child is destined to be the fall and rise of many in Israel, and a sign which shall be contradicted. And thy own soul a sword shall pierce, to contradict the thoughts of many."

After the ceremony of the presentation was over, the Blessed Mother kissed the hand of the priest and again asked his blessing. The same she did also to Anne, her former teacher. Then the Holy Family and the fourteen thousand angels in procession, ... returned to their lodging. They remained for some days in Jerusalem, in order to satisfy their devotion and during that time she spoke a few times with Simeon and Anne about the mysteries of the Redemption and of the prophecies. Both of them died shortly afterwards. The holy Family lodged at the expense of Simeon during these days.

12. The Holy Family flees to Egypt

When the Blessed Virgin Mary and St. Joseph returned from the Presentation of the Infant Jesus in the Temple, they decided to stay in Jerusalem for nine days in order to render fitting thanks for the blessing for which they had been chosen from among all men. The Blessed Mother had a special appreciation for the number nine, as her pregnancy lasted nine months.

On the fifth day of the novena after the presentation and purification, while the Blessed Mother was in the temple with the Baby Jesus in her arms, the Eternal Father spoke to Her and comforted her saying: "My Spouse and my Dove, thy wishes and intentions are pleasing in my eyes and I delight in them always. But you cannot finish the nine days devotion, which you have begun, for I have in store for thee other exercises of thy love. In order to save the life of thy Son and Mine, you must leave thy home and thy country, flee with Him and thy spouse Joseph into Egypt, where you are to remain until I shall decide otherwise: for Herod is seeking the life of the Child. The journey is long, most laborious and most fatiguing; you will suffer it all for My sake; for I am, and always will be, with Thee."

Answering, she said: "My God and Master, behold thy servant with a heart prepared to die for Thy love if necessary. Dispose of me according to Thy will. This only do I ask of Thy immense goodness, that, overlooking my want of merit and gratitude, Thou permit not my Son and Lord to suffer, and that Thou turn all pains and labor upon me, who am obliged to suffer them." The Almighty instructed her to follow St. Joseph's directions in all things concerning the journey.

That same night, while St. Joseph was asleep, the angel of the Most High appeared to him, and spoke to him as recorded by St. Matthew: "Arise, take the Child and His Mother and flee to Egypt; there you must remain until I return to give thee other advice; for Herod is seeking the Child in order to take away His life."

Immediately St. Joseph arose full of determination and sorrow. Entering her room, he said: "My Lady, God wills that we should be afflicted; for His holy angel has announced to me the pleasure and the decree of the Almighty, that we arise and flee with the Child into Egypt, because Herod is seeking to take away His life. Encourage thyself, my Lady, to bear the labors of this journey and tell me what I can do for thy comfort, since I hold my life and being at the service of thy Child and of Thee."

"My husband and my master," answered the Queen, "if we have received from the hands of the Most High such great blessings of grace, it is meant that we joyfully accept temporal afflictions (Job 2, 13). We bear with us the Creator of heaven and earth; if He has placed us so near to Him, what arms shall be able to harm us, even if it be the arm of Herod? Wherever we carry with us all our Good, the highest treasure of heaven …"

The Holy Family left Jerusalem and began their journey under the silence and obscurity of night. Their love for the Infant Jesus would naturally excite in them anxiety and suffering on an occasion like this. They did not know what would happen during such a long journey, nor when it should end, nor how they would survive in Egypt, where they would be entire strangers, nor what comfort or convenience they would find there for raising the Child, nor even how they would be able to ward off great sufferings from Him on the way to Egypt. Therefore their hearts were filled with many misgivings and anxious thoughts when they parted in so much haste from their lodging; but their sorrow was much relieved when their ten thousand angels again appeared to them in human forms and in their former splendor and beauty, and when their angels again changed the night into the brightest day for the Holy Family. As they departed from the city the holy angels humiliated themselves and adored the Incarnate Word in the arms of His Blessed Mother. All of the angels encouraged her by again offering their homage and service, stating that it was the will of the Most High that they guide and accompany them on this journey.

The Blessed Mother longed to visit again the place of the Nativity, in order to venerate the sacred cave and the crib, which had offered shelter and hospitality to her most holy Son at His entrance into the world. But the holy angels, knowing of her unspoken desires, said to her: "Our Queen and Lady, Mother of our Creator, it is very important to hurry on our journey without any delay; because of the escape of the Magi Kings and their failure to return to Jerusalem, and on account of the words spoken by the priest Simeon, and by Anne, the people have been roused to attention. Some of them have begun to say that you are the Mother of the Messiah and others say that thy Son is a Prophet. Various rumors have spread about concerning the visit of the Magi Kings in Bethlehem, and of all these things Herod is informed. He has commanded that you be sought after very carefully and consequently a most diligent search is being made to find you. On this account the Most High has commanded you to flee at night and with much haste."

The Blessed Mother yielded to the will of the Almighty made known to her by the holy angels. She therefore reverenced from afar the sacred place of the birth of her Holy Son, renewing the memory of the mysteries and the favors received in the cave. The holy angel who stood as guard of the sacred cave approached Them on their way in visible form and adored the Incarnate Word in the arms of His Mother. As she was allowed to see this angel and speak to him, the Blessed Mother rejoiced and was comforted. She would have also preferred to travel by way of Hebron; since it was only a short distance from the road they were now traveling, and Elisabeth was just at that time in that city with her son John. But the anxiety of St. Joseph prevented this diversion and delay; for he said to Mary: "My Lady, I think it is extremely important that we do not delay our journey even for one instant; and that we hurry as much as possible to flee from the place of danger. Therefore, it would not be prudent to go to Hebron, where they will find us more easily than in any other parts of the country." "Let it be according to thy pleasure," answered the humble Blessed Mother "yet I wish you give me permission to send one of my angels to Elisabeth, in order to inform my cousin of the cause of our flight, so that she herself may protect her son; for the wrath of Herod is so roused that it will extend to them."

The Blessed Virgin Mary knew of the design to murder the children; but She did not tell St. Joseph of it at that time. With the permission of St. Joseph, the Blessed Mother sent one of the principal angels of her guard, in order to notify St. Elisabeth of what Herod was about to do.

The angel, according to the order and pleasure of the Queen, proceeded to inform the fortunate and blessed Elisabeth of all these events as far as was proper. He told her that the Mother of God was fleeing from the wrath of Herod into Egypt, as this tyrant was now searching for the Child in order to kill Him. He warned her to see to the safety of saint John by hiding him in some place of refuge. He also manifested to her other mysteries of the Incarnate Word according to the command of the heavenly Mother. The holy Elisabeth was filled with joy and wonder at this message, and she expressed her desire to meet and adore the Infant Jesus, and to see his Mother; asking him whether they could be reached. The holy angel answered that his King and Lord was passing with his Mother at a distance from Hebron and could not wait for her visit. Elisabeth immediately sent a servant with some gifts consisting in provisions, money and material for clothing the Infant. She foresaw their needs in a strange country and instructed the servant to overtake them with all haste. He met them in Gaza, which lies a little less than twenty hours from Jerusalem, on the road from Israel to Egypt, not far from the Mediterranean Sea.

In this town of Gaza. they stayed two days, for St. Joseph and the donkey which carried the Blessed Mother and the Baby Jesus were exhausted and fatigued from the journey. From that place they sent back the servant of St. Elisabeth, cautioning him not to tell any one of their whereabouts. But God provided still more protection against this danger; for He took away from this man all remembrance of what St. Joseph had charged him to conceal, so that he retained only his message to St. Elisabeth. The Blessed Virgin Mary used the gifts sent by Elisabeth to help the poor; because she could not bear to pass them by unassisted. Of the cloth sent to her, she made a cloak for the Baby Jesus and one for St. Joseph, to shelter Them from the discomforts of the cold and of the journey.

She also used other things in their possession for the comfort of her Child and of St. Joseph. The prudent Blessed Mother would not rely on miraculous assistance whenever she could provide for the daily needs by her own diligence and labor, for in these matters she desired to subject herself to the natural order and depend upon her own efforts. During the two days which they spent in Gaza the most Blessed Mary performed some miraculous deeds. She freed two sick people from certain death and cured their ailments. She restored a crippled woman, the use of her limbs. On the third day after the Holy Family arrived in Gaza, they departed from that city for Egypt. Soon leaving the inhabited parts of Israel they traversed a sandy desert for one hundred fifty miles in order to arrive and take their abode in Heliopolis, the present city of Cairo in Egypt. This journey from Bethlehem to Egypt took fifty days. Their guardian angels informed them that the Almighty wanted them to live in the city of Heliopolis until He would tell them to return to Nazareth.

In order to understand how much Mary, Joseph and the Infant Jesus suffered on their pilgrimage, it must be remembered that the Almighty permitted His Onlybegotten Son, with His most holy Mother and saint Joseph, to suffer the inconveniences and hardships naturally connected with travel through this desert. And although Mary never complained, they each suffered many personal in conveniences and discomforts. According to the Blessed Virgin Mary, the gods of Egypt, Greece and Rome were real; they were all Lucifer's generals of the demonic armies. As Jesus passed by the Egyptians' places of worship, the idols crashed to the ground, the altars fell to pieces, and the temples crumbled to ruins. And the demons were hurled into hell. The Blessed Virgin Mary and St. Joseph knew this to be the work of the Incarnate Word. The demons felt the divine power but did not know its source.The Egyptian people were astounded at these inexplicable happenings; although among the more learned, ever since the sojourn of Jeremias in Egypt, an ancient tradition was current that a King of the Jews would come and that the temples of the idols would be destroyed. Yet of this prophecy the common people had no knowledge, nor did the learned know how it was to be fulfilled: and therefore the terror and confusion was spread among all of them, as was prophesied by Isaias (Is.9,1).

In this disturbance and fear, some, reflecting on these events, came to the Blessed Virgin Mary and St. Joseph; and, in their curiosity at seeing these strangers in their midst, they also spoke to them about the ruin of their temples and their idols. Making use of this occasion the Blessed Mother began to teach these people, speaking to them of the true God and instructing them that He is the one and only Creator of heaven and earth, who is alone to be adored, and acknowledged as God; that all others are false and demonic gods.

Because of these strange happenings resulting in so many of the demons being cast into hell by a new power, Lucifer was greatly disturbed. Furiously enraged, he came forth upon the earth in order to investigate the cause of these events. He roamed through all Egypt, where so many temples and altars of his idols had been destroyed; and reaching Heliopolis, the largest of the cities and the scene of the greatest destruction to his dominions, he sought to determine what kind of people were there. He found nothing new, except that the Blessed Virgin Mary had arrived in the city. Of the Infant Jesus he gave no consideration deeming Him a child just like all the rest of that age, for he knew nothing particular about Him. But as he had been so often vanquished by the virtues and holiness of the Blessed Mother, he was seized with new anxiety; although he considered a woman far too insignificant for such great works, yet he resolved anew to persecute her and to stir up against her his demons.

He therefore returned immediately to hell and, calling a meeting of his princes of darkness, told them of the destruction of the temples and idols in Egypt. For these demons had been hurled by the divine power from their habitations with such suddenness, confusion and torment that at their departure they were unable to determine the destruction of the idols and temples which they were forced to leave. Lucifer, informing them of all that had happened, and that he feared the destruction of his reign in Egypt, told them that he could not understand what was the cause of this ruin, since he had found there only that Woman, his enemy (for so the dragon called most holy Mary); and though he knew that her power was extraordinary, yet he did not presume it to be so great to account for their calamities.

Nevertheless, he wanted them to begin a new war against her, and that all should prepare themselves for battle. Lucifer's demons proclaimed their readiness to obey, trying to console him in his desperate fury and promising him victory, as if their forces were as great as their arrogance (Is. 16, 6).

Many legions of devils came forth from hell and went to the place where the Blessed Virgin Mary was at that time. As they suspected that God had used her as His instrument to cause all their losses in Egypt; the devils thought they could make up for their defeat and restore their dominion if they succeeded in overcoming her. But they were astonished to find that when they attempted to approach her in order to begin their diabolical attacks they could not come nearer to her than a distance of two thousand paces; for they were restrained by the divine power, which they perceived was coming from the Blessed Virgin Mary herself. Although Lucifer and his demonic legions struggled violently, they were paralyzed and as if bound in strong and tormenting shackles, without being able to reach the most unconquerable Queen; while Mary witnessed their struggles, holding in her arms the omnipotence of God himself. As Lucifer persevered in his attempts, he was suddenly hurled into the abyss of hell with all his squadrons and wicked spirits. This defeat and ruin filled the dragon with vast torment and anxiety, and as the like had overtaken him repeatedly since the Incarnation, he began to have new misgivings, whether the Messiah had not come into the world. But since he knew nothing of the mystery, and expected the Messiah to come in great splendor and renown, he remained in uncertainty and doubt, full of tormenting fury and wrath. He was consumed with the desire to find out the cause of his sufferings, and the more he inquired the more was he involved in darkness and so much the less did he ascertain of the true cause.

13. Holy Family's Life in Egypt

During the whole of this first year his sweetest Mother had wrapped the infant God in clothes and coverings usual with other children; for He did not wish to be distinguished in this from others, and He wished to bear witness to his true humanity and to his love for mortals, enduring this inconvenience otherwise not required of Him. The most prudent Mother, judging that now the time had come to free Him from swaddling clothes and place Him on his feet, knelt down before the Child in its cradle and said: "My Son and sweetest Love of my soul, my Lord, I desire, as thy slave, to be punctual in fulfilling thy wishes. O, Light of my eyes, Thou hast been for a long time oppressed by the swaddling-clothes and thereby gone to the extreme of thy love for men; it is time Thou change this manner. Tell me, my Master, what shall I do to place Thee on thy feet?"

"My Mother," answered the Infant Jesus, "… Clothe Me, my Mother, in a tunic of a lowly and ordinary color. This alone will I wear, and it shall grow with Me. Over this garment shall they cast lots at my death (Ps. 21, 19); for even this shall not be left at my disposal, but at the disposal of others; so that men shall see that I was born and wish to live poor and destitute ... … I will wear an ordinary covering for my feet until the time of my public preaching shall come, for this I must do barefooted. But I do not wish to wear linen, because it can cause carnal pleasures, and is the cause of many vices in men. I wish to teach many by my example to renounce possessions for love and imitation of Me."

Immediately the great Queen set diligently about fulfilling the will of her most holy Son. Procuring some wool in its natural and uncolored state, She spun it very finely with her own hands and of it She wove a garment of one piece and without any seam, similar to knitted stuff, or rather like twilled cloth, for it was woven of twisted cords, not like smooth-woven goods. She wove it upon a small loom, by meshes, crocheting it of one seamless piece in a mysterious manner (John 19, 23).

Two things were wonderful about it: that it was entirely even and uniform, without any seams, and that, at her request, the natural color was changed to a more suitable one, which was a mixture of brown and a most exquisite silver-gray, so that it could not be called either, appearing to be neither altogether brown, nor silvery, nor gray, but having a mixture of them all. She also wove a pair of sandals of strong thread, like hempen shoes, with which She covered the feet of the infant God. Besides these She made a half tunic of linen, which was to serve as an undergarment. In the next chapter I shall tell what happened when She clothed the Infant Jesus.

At this time occurred the anniversary of the Incarnation and of the Nativity of the divine Word, both of them when they had already settled in Egypt. The celestial Queen celebrated these feasts, so joyous for the Mother of God, commencing a custom observed by Her during all the rest of her life.

St. Joseph took a small amount of the gold with them which he used to purchase a little house for their home in Egypt. He would make pieces of furniture to sell to provide for the Holy Family's food. They grew some fruits and vegetables on a tiny plot of ground next to their home. Jesus would help in small matters with St. Joseph's projects.

When Jesus was four years old, He went out every day to preach and to heal the sick and the Blessed Virgin Mary did the same; but they conducted their daily missions separately. At early evening, they all returned home to have supper together. Contrary to popular thoughts, Jesus was not a carpenter but a preacher all His life.

14. Holy Family's Life in Nazareth

The Child Jesus was seven years old when the Eternal Father announced that it was time to return to Nazareth. This decree the Eternal Father intimated to His most holy Son on a certain day in the presence of His holy Mother and while she was with Him in prayer. ... That very night the angel of the Eternal Father spoke to St. Joseph in his sleep, as Matthew relates (Matt. 2, 19), "Arise Joseph and take the Child and His Mother and return to your home in Nazareth for Herod and those with him that had sought the life of the Child, are dead."

St. Joseph immediately told the Child Jesus and His Mother of the command of the Eternal Father and they both answered, that the will of the heavenly Father must be done. Thereupon they resolved upon their journey without delay, immediately distributing among the poor the little furniture contained in their dwelling. Their house the Holy Family lived in for seven years was left in the possession of certain of the most devout and pious persons in Heliopolis.

They departed for Israel in the company of their ten thousand angels. The Blessed Mother sat on the donkey with the Divine Child on her lap and St. Joseph walked along side.
After the Holy Family had returned to their house in Nazareth, the time of the year in which the Jews were obliged to present themselves before the Lord God in the temple of Jerusalem, was at hand. This commandment obliged the Jews to this duty three times each year; but it obliged only the men, not the women. The women could go or not, according to their devotion, for it was neither commanded nor prohibited to them. The Blessed Mother and St. Joseph decided they should go in this regard.

They finally arranged, that two times a year saint Joseph was to go to Jerusalem by himself, while on the third occasion They would go together. The trip would last seven days. And when the Holy Family went together, the ten thousand angels accompanied the three pilgrims, Jesus, Mary and Joseph, in human forms, in their radiance and reverence, serving their Creator and their Queen.

The distance between Nazareth and Jerusalem was approximately 75 miles and the holy angels, according to the command and disposition of Jesus walked with them going and returning.

They consumed more time in these journeys than in previous ones; for after they had come back from Egypt the Child Jesus desired that they journey on foot; and therefore all three of the Holy Family made the pilgrimage afoot. It was necessary to go slowly because the Child Jesus tired easily. Jesus refused to make use of His power to lessen the difficulties of the journey, but undertook it as a man subject to suffering and allowed all the natural causes to produce their effects. One of these effects was the fatigue and exhaustion caused by travel. Although this was Jesus' first journey and the Blessed Mother and St. Joseph eased His fatigue by sometimes carrying Him in their arms; yet this was but a slight alleviation and later on He always made the whole journey on foot. Ordinarily she led Him by the hand, and sometimes this was also done by St. Joseph. Very often the wind would flutter through the hair of the Child Jesus as He walked along. Jesus' hair grew to no greater length than was necessary and He lost none of it, except during His Passion when the executioners tore out His hair and beard. In all her interior and exterior conduct, the Blessed Mother was wonderful to the angels and pleasing to her most holy Son Jesus.

During these journeys of the Holy Family, Jesus and Mary performed heroic works of charity for the benefit of souls; They converted many to the knowledge of God and freed them from their sins and justified them, instructing them regarding salvation. At the age of twelve Jesus traveled with Mary and Joseph to the Temple of Jerusalem for the seven day feast of Passover. Upon their return, Mary presumed that Jesus was with Joseph and Joseph presumed that Jesus was with His Blessed Mother. Thus assured, Mary and Joseph traveled for home an entire day, as saint Luke tells us. As the pilgrims proceeded onwards they gradually thinned out, each taking his own direction and joining again with his wife or family. The most holy Mary and St. Joseph found themselves at length in the place where they had agreed to meet on the first evening after leaving Jerusalem.

When the Blessed Mother saw that Jesus was not with St. Joseph and when Joseph saw that Jesus was not with His Mother, the two were struck dumb with amazement and were surprised. Both felt overwhelmed with their remissness in watching over their most holy Son and thus blamed themselves for his absence; for neither of them had any suspicion of the mysterious manner in which He had been able to elude their vigilance. After a time they recovered somewhat from their astonishment and with deepest sorrow took counsel with each other as to what was to be done (Luke 2, 45). The loving Mother said to saint Joseph: "My spouse and my master, my heart cannot rest, unless we return with all haste to Jerusalem in order to seek my most holy Son." This they proceeded to do, beginning their search among their relations and friends, of whom, however, none could give them any information or any comfort in their sorrow ; on the contrary their answers only increased their anxiety, since none of them had so much as seen their Son since their departure from Jerusalem.

The distraught Mother turned to her holy angels that accompanied her and the other nine thousand were with Jesus; this was the order maintained whenever Jesus was separated from His Mother. She asked her angels saying: "My friends and companions, you well know the cause of my sorrow: in this bitter affliction be my consolation and give me some information concerning my Beloved Jesus so that I may seek and find Him. ..."

The holy angels never lost sight of Jesus, were aware that the Lord wished to furnish His Mother this occasion of great merit, and that it was not yet time to reveal the secret to her, answered by speaking to her words of consolation without manifesting to her the whereabouts and the doings of their Lord Jesus.

This evasive answer raised new doubts in the Blessed Mother. Her anxiety caused her to breakout in tears and sighs of grief, and urged her onward in search of Jesus.

84

The Blessed Mother then began to discuss within her heart the different possibilities. Her first thought was the fear that Archelaus, son of Herod, might have noticed the presence of Jesus and have taken Him prisoner. Although she knew from the Holy Scriptures and revelations, and by her conversations with her most holy Son and Teacher, that the time for his Passion and Death had not yet come, but that Jesus might have been taken prisoner.

The Blessed Virgin Mary persevered in her tears and dismay without cessation or rest, without sleeping or eating anything for three whole days. Although the angels accompanied her in corporeal forms and witnessed her affliction and sorrow, they gave her no clue to find her lost Child.

On the third day the Blessed Mother began to believe more firmly, that Jesus was with St. John. When She was about to execute her resolve and was on the point of departing for the desert, the holy angels detained her, urging her not to undertake the journey, since Jesus was not there. She wanted also to go to Bethlehem, in the hope of finding Him in the cave of the Nativity, but this the holy angels likewise prevented, telling her that Jesus was near. Although the Blessed Mother heard these answers and well perceived that the holy angels knew His whereabouts; but she understood that God had a lesson or purpose in concealing Himself and because of her humility she would not ask her angels again.

During these three days the Almighty left the Blessed Mother to her natural resources of nature and of grace, deprived of her power, special privileges and favors; for, with the exception of the company and conversations with her angels, God suspended all of her power and other blessings familiar to her. In the temple the Child Jesus while seeming to ask questions taught the scribes with a divine efficacy. The scribes and learned men who heard Him were all dumbfounded. Convinced by His arguments they looked at each other and in great astonishment asked: "What miracle is this? and what prodigy of a boy! Whence has He come and who is the Child?"

But though thus astonished, they did not recognize or suspect who it was, that thus taught and enlightened them concerning such an important truth. During this time and before Jesus had finished his argument, His Blessed Mother and St. Joseph arrived, just in time to hear him advance his last arguments. When He had finished, all the teachers of the law arose with stupendous amazement. The Blessed Mother absorbed in joy, approached her most loving Son and in the presence of the whole assembly, spoke to Him the words recorded by St. Luke: "Son, why have You done this to us? Your father and I have been searching for You."

Jesus answered: "Why were you looking for Me? Did you not know that I must be about My Father's business?"

Together, Jesus, Mary and Joseph returned to their home in Nazareth. And Jesus was submissive to His Blessed Mother and St. Joseph. Jesus would go out every day among people to preach and heal the sick. The Blessed Virgin Mary would do the same but alone. St. Joseph would work as a carpenter making items of furniture for sale to support the Holy Family. Jesus passed the period of His adolescence from age twelve to eighteen and His Blessed Mother reached her perfect growth in her thirty-third year.

At the age of thirty-three years the body has fully developed, being the end of youthful vigor and the beginning of the aging process. On this account our Lord Jesus Christ died at the completion of his thirty-third year; for His most ardent love induced Him to wait only until His body attained maturity with maximum vigor and was most capable of bringing the perfect gifts of nature and grace to His sacrifice. In accordance with this the Almighty created Adam and Eve in the condition of a man and woman at the age of thirty-three years.

The Blessed Virgin Mary at the time of her thirty-third year, her virginal body had attained full natural growth, so well-proportioned and beautiful, that she was the admiration not only of human beings, but of the angelic spirits themselves. She had grown in size and stature to the most perfect proportion in all the parts of her body and most strikingly resembled her divine Son in features and complexion, when later on He arrived at that age; always, of course, taking into account, that Christ was the most perfect Man, while His Mother was the most perfect Woman.

Other human mortals at age thirty-three ordinarily begin to deteriorate and gradually approach decay as far as their body is concerned; the hair begins to whiten, the skin starts to wrinkle, the strength weakens, and the human body commences to decline toward old age and corruption. But in the Blessed Virgin Mary it was not so; her wonderful beauty and strength, which she had attained at the age of thirty-three years, remained unchanged; and when she had reached her seventieth year, she still retained the same beauty and entirety of her virginal body as at the age of thirty-three.

The Blessed Virgin Mary was well aware of this special privilege given to her by the Most High and she rendered Him most humble thanks. She understood also that it was granted to her in order that the likeness of her most holy Son might always be preserved in her, though with the differences consequent upon her different nature and longer life; for the Lord Jesus attained full bodily growth at thirty-three years, while she retained it during her much longer life.

At the age of fifty-two St. Joseph's health and well-being had started to decline and his bodily strength gradually diminished. In like manner, the care and attention of the thirty-three year old Blessed Virgin Mary assisting and serving him with punctuality increased. He was broken down and worn out as far as his body was concerned. Because of his journeys and his challenging labors for the sustenance of the Holy Family, he had weakened much more than his years. The Blessed Virgin Mary knew that St. Joseph was significantly weakened and served him better than any wife ever did her husband, spoke to him and said: "My spouse, I am deeply obliged to you for your faithful labors, watchfulness and care you have taken for my welfare. By the sweat of your brow you have until now supported me and my holy Son, the true God, and in this dedication, you have spent your strength and your health and your life in protecting me and attending upon my welfare. …"

"... From the hands of the Almighty you will receive the reward for your works and the blessings which you deserve. But now I insist that you rest from your labors since your strength is gone. I wish from now on to show my gratitude by laboring for you and Jesus and to provide for our sustenance as the Almighty wishes us to have."

St. Joseph listened to the words of his Blessed Spouse with abundant tears of humblest acknowledgment and consolation. Although he at first earnestly entreated her to allow him to continue forever in his labors, yet at last he yielded to her request and obeyed his Spouse, the Mother of God. From that time on he rested from hard labor of his hands, by which he had earned a livelihood for all three of them. They gave away the carpenter tools as an alms, not wishing to have anything superfluous or useless in their house and family. Being thus at leisure, St. Joseph occupied himself entirely in contemplative prayer. He had happiness and good fortune of continually enjoying the sight and conversations with Jesus and Mary. The Blessed Mother and Jesus attended to St. Joseph and nursed him in his sickness, consoling and sustaining him with the greatest patience. St. Joseph accepted their assistance with humility, reverence, gratitude and love. And he thus became the admiration and joy of the angels and the pleasure and delight of the Most High.

At that time, the Blessed Mother took it upon herself to work to support Jesus and St. Joseph. At the age of thirty-three years she showed her strength purchasing a field and cultivating the vineyard by her own labor to bring forth its fruits. St. Joseph confided in her, and Jesus confided in her as well, and they were not deceived. Mary began to busy herself much more in spinning and weaving linen and wool.

The last three years of his life St. Joseph was a complete invalid with certain sicknesses, such as fever, violent headaches and very painful arthritis which greatly afflicted and weakened him. At this time, Jesus and Mary had to carry him from his couch which he slept upon to the chair at the table where they ate. They washed him and dressed him daily.

St. Joseph died at the age of sixty years and a few days. At the age of thirty-three St. Joseph married the Blessed Virgin Mary who was fourteen. They lived together as virgins with separate rooms for a little longer than twenty-seven years. When St. Joseph died, the Blessed Virgin Mary was forty-one and a half. She felt the natural sorrow due to the death of St. Joseph; for she loved him as her spouse, as a man preeminent in perfection and holiness, as her protector and benefactor. At the age of thirty-three the Blessed Virgin Mary remained without further aging for her entire life. She showed no signs of decline, or of more advanced age, or of weakness, but always remained in that same most perfect state of womanhood as a thirty-three year old.

After the death of St. Joseph, Jesus and Mary lived together for four years before suffering His passion and death.

15. Jesus' Public Life

i. Baptism of Jesus

John the Baptist had been enlightened in great mysteries. He was commanded to go forth to preach and baptize. All of these mysteries were manifested to him anew and with greater clearness and abundance on the occasion when he was notified that the Savior of the world was coming to be baptized.

Jesus joined the multitudes and as one of the rest asked Baptism of St. John. The Baptist knew Him and, falling at his feet, hesitated, saying: "I have need of being baptized, and You, Lord, asks Baptism of me?" as is recorded by St. Matthew. But the Savior answered: "Suffer it to be so now. For so it becomes us to fulfill all justice" (Matt. 3, 14). By thus hesitating to baptize Jesus Christ his Lord and asking Him for Baptism instead, he gave evidence that he recognized Him as the true Redeemer and there is no contradiction between this and what the Evangelist St. John records of St. John the Baptist as saying to the Jews: "And I knew Him not; but He who sent me to baptize with water said to me: He, upon whom you shall see the Holy Spirit descending, and remaining, He it is that baptizes with the Holy Spirit. And I saw, and I gave testimony that this is the Son of God" (John1, 33, 34). There is also no contradiction between these words of St. John and those of St. Matthew; for the testimony of the Eternal Father's voice over Jesus on the banks of the Jordan happened when St. John the Baptist had the vision of Jesus coming to be baptized. John had not seen Jesus Christ bodily until then and could, therefore, deny having known Christ, at least in the same way as he then knew Him; for just because he knew Jesus Christ then both by sight and by intellectual vision.

When St. John had finished baptizing our Lord, the heavens opened and the Holy Spirit descended visibly in the form of a dove upon Jesus' head and the voice of His Father was heard: "This is my beloved Son, in whom I am well pleased" (Matt. 3, 17). Many of the bystanders heard this voice, namely, those who were not unworthy of such a wonderful favor; they also saw the Holy Spirit descending upon Jesus the Savior.

This was the most convincing proof which could ever be given of the Divinity of the Savior, as well on the part of the Father, who acknowledged Him as His Son, as also in regard to the nature of the testimony given; for without any reserve was Jesus manifested as the true God, equal to His Eternal Father in substance and in perfection. The Father Himself wished to be the first to testify to the Divinity of Jesus in order that by virtue of His testimony all the other witnesses might be ratified. There was also another mystery in this voice of the Eternal Father: it was as it were a restoration of the honor of His Son before the world and a recompense for His having thus humiliated Himself by receiving the Baptism of the remission of sins, though He was entirely free from fault and never could have upon Him the guilt of sin (Heb. 7, 26). Jesus humiliating Himself in this baptism of sins, sought and obtained from the Eternal Father a general pardon for all those who were to receive it; He freed them from the power of Satan and of sin, and regenerated them into a new existence as spiritual adopted sons of the Most High, brethren of their Redeemer and Lord. The past, present and future sins of men always remaining in the sight of the Eternal Father, had prevented the effects of this Baptism; but Jesus our Lord merited the application of this remedy, so that the Eternal Father was obliged to accept it in justice as a complete satisfaction according to all the requirements of His equity.

ii. Jesus fasts for forty days and Satan tempts Him

Without delay Christ our Lord pursued his journey from the Jordan to the desert after His Baptism. Only his holy angels attended and accompanied Him, serving and worshipping Him, singing the divine praises on account of what He was now about to undertake for the salvation of mankind. He came to the place chosen by Him for his fast; a desert spot among bare ground and rocks, where there was also a hidden cavern. Here He stopped and chose it for His habitation during the days of His fast (Matt. 4, 1). In deepest humility He prostrated Himself upon the ground which was always the method of beginning His prayer and that of His most Blessed Mother. He praised the Eternal Father and gave Him thanks for the works of His divine right hand and for having according to His pleasure given Him this cave to rest.

In a suitable manner He thanked even this desert for accepting His presence and keeping Him hidden from the world during the time He was to spend there fasting and praying. He continued His prayers prostrate in the form of a cross, and this was His most frequent position in the desert; for in this manner He often prayed to the Eternal Father for the salvation of men. During these prayers, He sometimes sweated blood.

Many of the wild beasts of the desert came to the place now inhabited by their Creator; for He sometimes walked about in these regions. With an admirable instinct they recognized Him and gave forth their voices, moving about as if in testimony of His Divinity. The birds of the sky came in great multitudes gathered around the Savior, were especially eager in their demonstrations, manifesting their joy at the blessed presence of their divine King and Lord by their sweet and loud singing and in diverse other ways.

After the Savior had begun his fast He persevered therein without eating anything for forty days, offering up his fast to the eternal Father as a satisfaction for the disorder and sins to which men are drawn by the so vile and debasing, yet so common and even so much esteemed vice of gluttony. Just as our Lord overcame this vice so He also vanquished all the rest, and He made recompense to the eternal Judge and supreme Legislator for the injuries perpetrated through these vices by men. According to the enlightenment vouchsafed to me, our Savior, in order to assume the office of Preacher and Teacher and to become our Mediator and Redeemer before the Father, thus vanquished all the vices of mortals and He satisfied the offenses committed through them by the exercises of the virtues contrary to them, just as He did in regard to gluttony. Although He continued this exercise during all his life with the most ardent charity, yet during His fast He directed in a special manner all His efforts toward this purpose.

A loving Father, whose sons have committed great crimes for which they are to endure the most horrible punishment, sacrifices all his possessions in order to ward off their impending fate; so our most loving Father and Brother, Jesus Christ, wished to pay our debts.

In satisfaction for our pride He offered his profound humility; for our avarice, his voluntary poverty and total privation of all that was his, for our base and lustful inclinations, his penance and austerity; for our hastiness and vengeful anger, his meekness and charity toward his enemies; for our negligence and laziness, his divine efforts.

Jesus prayed to the Eternal Father from His inmost soul, to which the intelligence of the demon could not penetrate, saying: "My Father and Eternal God, I now enter into battle with the enemy in order to crush his power and humble his pride and his malice against my beloved souls. For thy glory and for the benefit of souls I submit to the daring presumption of Lucifer. I wish thereby to crush his head in order that when mortal men are attacked by his temptations without their fault, they may find his arrogance already broken. I beseech Thee My Father, to remember My battle and victory in favor of mortals attacked by the common enemy. Strengthen their weakness through My triumph, let them obtain victory; let them be encouraged by My example, and let them learn from Me how to resist and overcome their enemies."

During this battle the holy angels that attended upon Christ were hidden from the sight of Lucifer, in order that he might not begin to understand and suspect the divine power of our Savior. The holy angels gave glory and praise to the Father and the Holy Spirit, who rejoiced in the works of the Incarnate Word. The Blessed Virgin Mary from her oratory witnessed the battle in the following manner. The temptation of Jesus began on the thirty-fifth day of His fast in the desert, and lasted for five days until the end of His fast, as related by the Evangelists. Lucifer assumed the shape of a man and presented himself before Jesus as a stranger, who had never seen or known Him before. He clothed himself in brilliant light, like that of an angel, and thought that Jesus after His long fast must be suffering great hunger, Lucifer said to Jesus: "If Thou be the Son of God, command that these stones be made into bread" (Matt. 4, 3).

By his cunning advice on the possibility of Jesus being the Son of God, the demon sought some information on what was giving him the greatest concern. But Jesus answered only with a few words: "Not by bread alone does man live, but by every word from the mouth of God." Lucifer did not understand the meaning of Jesus' words but thought Him to mean that God could sustain the life of man without bread or any other nourishment.

Lucifer found himself repulsed by the force of this answer and by the hidden power which accompanied it; but he wished to show no weakness, nor desist from this confrontation. The Lord Jesus allowed the demon to continue in his temptation and for this purpose permitted the devil to carry His body to Jerusalem and to be placed on the pinnacle of the temple. Here Jesus could see multitudes of people, though He himself was not seen by anybody. Lucifer tried to arouse in Jesus the Lord the vain desire of casting Himself down from this high place, so that the crowds of men, seeing Him unhurt, might proclaim Him as a great and wonderful man of God. Again using the words of the holy Scriptures, Lucifer said to Him: "If Thou be the Son of God, cast Thyself down, for it is written (Ps. 90, 11): that He has given his angels charge over Thee, and in their hands they shall bear Thee up, so that Thou will not dash Thy foot against a stone" (Matt. 4, 6). The holy angels who accompanied Jesus their King, were full of wonder, that He should permit Lucifer to carry Him bodily in his hands, solely for the benefit of mortal man. With Lucifer were innumerable demons; for on that occasion hell was almost emptied of its inhabitants in order to furnish Lucifer assistance for this battle. Jesus answered: "It is also written: Thou shalt not tempt the Lord thy God." While giving these answers Jesus showed an unequaled meekness, profound humility, and a majesty so superior to all the attempts of Lucifer, as was of itself alone sufficient to crush Lucifer's arrogance and to cause him torments and confusion never felt before.

After this failure Lucifer attacked the Lord Jesus in still another way, seeking to rouse His ambition by offering Him some share in his dominion.

For this purpose, he took Jesus to a high mountain, from which could be seen many lands, and said to Him with deceitful cunning: "All these will I give to Thee, if falling down, Thou wilt adore me" (Matt. 4, 9).

Jesus the King and Lord answered: "Be gone, Satan! for it is written: For only the Lord thy God thou shalt adore, and Him only shalt thou serve." By this command, "Be gone Satan!" Jesus the Redeemer took away from Lucifer permission to tempt Him further, and hurled him and all his legions into the deepest abysses of hell. There they found themselves entirely crushed and buried in its deepest caverns, unable to move for three days. When they were permitted again to rise, seeing themselves vanquished and annihilated, they began to assume that Jesus might be the Incarnate Son of God. In this doubt and uncertainty they remained, without ever being able to come to certain conviction until the death of Jesus the Savior. Lucifer was overcome by hellish wrath at his defeat and was almost consumed by his own fury.

Then Jesus sang hymns of praise and thanks to the Eternal Father for having given Him this triumph over the common enemy of God and man; and amidst the triumphal songs a multitude of angels came forth and carried Him back to the desert. The angels carried Him in their hands, although He had no need of their help, since He could make use of his own divine power; but this service of the angels was due to Him in recompense for enduring the audacity of Lucifer in carrying Him to the pinnacle of the temple and to the mountain top. It would never have entered into the thoughts of man, that the Lord God should give such permission to Satan, if it had not been made known in the Gospels.

iii. Jesus calls five of His Apostles

After His fast Jesus visited the villages in Judea for ten months. For the time had arrived to publicly proclaim Himself as the Messiah. Jesus went to the Jordan River to allow St. John to testify that Jesus was the Messiah. By divine revelation John the Baptist knew of this visit of Jesus and of His intention to make Himself known to the world as the Redeemer and the true Son of the Eternal Father.

Therefore, when St. John the Baptist saw Jesus coming he exclaimed in a loud voice to his disciples: "Ecce Agnus Dei!" "Behold the Lamb of God." This testimony referred not only to his previous identical words in regard to Jesus but also presupposed the specific instructions which he had given to his close disciples.

The two first disciples of Jesus who were with St. John the Baptist at the time, heard this testimony and, moved by it and by the light and grace interiorly given to them, began to follow Jesus. Kindly turning to them Jesus asked them, what they sought (John 1, 38). They answered that they wished to know where He lived; and Jesus invited them to follow. They went with Him that day. One was St. Andrew and the other was the youth St. John. St. Andrew and St. John were the first of St. John the Baptist's followers and first to follow Jesus as a result of John the Baptist's testimony without being outwardly called by Jesus. St. Andrew immediately sought his brother Simon and took him along, saying that he had found the Messiah. Looking upon Simon, Jesus said: "Thou art Simon the son of Jonah: thou shall be called Cephas, which is rendered Peter." All this happened within Judea and on the next day Jesus entered Galilee. There He found Philip and called him to follow. Philip immediately sought Nathanael and brought him to Jesus, telling him what had happened and that they had found the Messiah in the Person of Jesus of Nazareth. Nathanael believed because Jesus told him that He saw him lying under the fig tree.

With these five apostles were the first stones in the foundation of the new Church. These five went with Jesus throughout Galilee for the purpose of beginning His public preaching and baptizing. In these Apostles, He enkindled, from the moment of their joining Him, a new light and fire of divine love and showered on them His blessings.

96

iv. Jesus performs His first public miracle

This miracle of changing water into wine took place on the same day on which a year ago had happened the Baptism of Jesus by St. John the Baptist. This day was also the anniversary of the adoration of the Magi Kings. Therefore, there are three celebrations on the same day, the sixth of January. Jesus had just celebrated His thirtieth birthday, twelve days before.

The evangelist, St. John reports that after arriving in Galilee: "And the third day, there was a marriage in Cana of Galilee; and the Mother of Jesus was there. And Jesus and His disciples were also invited to the marriage." (John 2, 1). This history in "Ciudad de Dios" and that of the Gospels coincided with each other, and that the course of events was as follows:

At table Jesus and His Mother Mary ate of some of the food, but with the greatest moderation; yet also without showing outwardly their great abstinence. Although when They were alone They did not eat these types of food. Jesus commanded His disciples and Apostles to eat of what was placed before them on their evangelical tours of preaching and not to show any singularity in their way of life, such as is indulged in by the imperfect and those little versed in the paths of virtue; for the truly poor and humble must not presume to have a choice in their victuals. By divine arrangement and in order to give occasion to the miracle, the wine ran out during the meal and Mary said to Jesus: "They have no wine." And Jesus answered: "Woman, what is that to Me and to thee? My hour is not yet come." The Blessed Virgin Mary well understood this mystery and She said to the servants: "Do whatever He tells you." Then Jesus ordered the servants to fill the stone jars with water. All having been filled, the Lord bade them draw some of the wine into which the water had been changed, and bring it to the chief steward of the feast, who was at the head of the table and was one of the priests of the Law. When this one had tasted of the wine, he called the bridegroom in surprise and said to him: "Every man at first serves the good wine, and when men have drunk their fill then wine of a lesser quality Is served, but you have kept the best wine until now."

The chief steward knew nothing of the miracle when he tasted of the wine; because he sat at the head of the table, while Jesus and His Mother Mary with His disciples occupied the lower end of the table. ... Then the miracle of changing the water into wine and the dignity of Jesus was revealed. The disciples had their faith in Jesus confirmed again. Not only they, but many of the others that were present, believed that He was the true Messiah and they followed Him to the City of Capernaum from Cana with His Mother and disciples.

From Cana in Galilee to Capernaum, Jesus, Mary and His disciples walked. Capernaum was a large populous city near the sea of Galilee. According to St. John (John 2, 12), Jesus remained a few days.

v. Execution of John the Baptist

John the Baptist reprimanded Herod for his adulterous life taking his brother's wife Herodias for his wife. Because of this St. John was taken prisoner.

The birthday of Herod was to be celebrated by a banquet and ball, given by him to the nobles of Galilee, of which he was king. The degraded Herodias brought her daughter to the feast, in order to dance before the guests. King Herod was so taken in by the dancing girl that he promised her any gift or favor she desired, even if it were the half of his kingdom. She, directed by her mother asked for the head of John the Baptist, and that it be given to her immediately on a plate. Herod commanded it to be done because of the oath he had taken. During the imprisonment of St. John brought about by Herodias, he was much favored by the angels sent to him by Jesus and Mary.

The Blessed Mother tearfully asked Jesus to assist his cousin St. John in that hour, to comfort and console him before his death. Jesus responded to her request with much pleasure, saying that He would fulfill it entirely and bidding Her immediately to accompany Him on a visit to St. John. Then Jesus and his holy Mother Mary were miraculously transported to the dungeon cell where St. John lay fettered in chains and wounded in many parts of his body from scourgings order by Herodias.

As soon as St. John saw Jesus and Mary before him in the midst of the multitude of angels his chains fell from him and his wounds were healed. Jesus and Mary remained for some time. While engaged in conversation, three servants of Herod entered his prison cell ready to execute him. St. John presented his neck and the executioner cut off his head. Jesus and Mary were invisible to the executioners. But at the same moment Jesus received in His arms the body of St. John while Mary held St. John's head in her hands, both of Them offering this victim to the Eternal Father on the altar of their sacred hands. This was possible not only because the two Sovereigns of the world were invisible, but also because the servants of Herod had begun to quarrel as to which of them should flatter the infamous dancer and her mother by bringing them the head of St. John. In their dispute, without noticing the body and severed head suspended in air, the executioners snatched the head from the hands of the Blessed Virgin Mary and the rest of them followed in order to offer it on a plate to the daughter of Herodias. The sacred soul of St. John the Baptist, in the company of a multitude of angels, was sent to limbo, and its arrival renewed the joy of the holy souls imprisoned there. Jesus and Mary returned to the place they came from.

vi. Transfiguration of Jesus

Jesus had already spent more than two and a half years in preaching and performing miracles, and He was approaching the time predestined by the Eternal Father for satisfying divine justice, for redeeming the human race through His Passion and Death and thus to return to His Eternal Father. Since all His works were ordered with the highest wisdom for our instruction and salvation, the Lord resolved to prepare and strengthen some of His Apostles for the scandal of His Passion by manifesting to them beforehand in its glory that same body, which He was so soon to exhibit in the disfigurement of the Cross. Thus would they be reassured by the thought, that they had seen it transfigured in glory before they looked upon it disfigured by His sufferings.

This he had promised a short time before in the presence of all, although not to all, but only to some of his disciples, as is recorded by St. Matthew (Matt. 16, 28). For His Transfiguration He selected a high mountain in the center of Galilee, five miles east of Nazareth and called Mount Tabor. Ascending to its highest summit with three Apostles, Peter, and the two brothers James and John, He was transfigured before them. (Matt. 17,1; Mark 9, 1; Luke 9, 28).

The three Evangelists tell us that besides these Apostles, were present also the two prophets, Moses and Elias, discoursing with Jesus about His Passion, and that, while He was transfigured, a voice resounded from heaven of the Eternal Father, saying: "This is my beloved Son, in whom I am well pleased, listen to Him."

At the same time in which some of the holy angels were commissioned to bring the soul of Moses and Elias from their abode, others of her own guard carried the Blessed Virgin Mary to Mount Tabor, in order to witness the Transfiguration of her divine Son.

It was proper to fortify Her by this favor against the torments in store for her most holy soul. Moreover, she was to remain on earth as the Teacher of the holy Church, therefore it was proper that She should be one of the eye-witnesses of this great mystery.

vii. Jesus raises Lazarus

Jesus continued to perform miracles in Judea. Among them was the resurrection of Lazarus in Bethany, when He had been called by the two sisters, Martha and Mary. As this miracle took place so near to Jerusalem, the report of it was soon spread throughout the city. The priests and Pharisees, being irritated by this miracle, held a council (John 9, 17), in which they resolved upon the death of Jesus and commanded all those that had any knowledge of His whereabouts, to make it known; for after the resurrection of Lazarus, Jesus retired to the town of Ephrem, until the proximate feast of the Pasch should arrive.

100

As the time of celebrating it by his own Death drew nigh, He showed Himself more openly with His twelve Apostles; and He told them privately that they should now get themselves ready to go to Jerusalem, where the Son of man, He himself, should be delivered over to the chiefs of the Pharisees, bound as a prisoner, scourged, and ill-treated unto the death of the Cross (Matt. 20, 18). In the meanwhile the priests kept a sharp watch to find Him among those who came to celebrate the Pasch. Six days prior to the Passover feast Jesus again visited Bethany, where He had called Lazarus to life, and where He was entertained by the two sisters. They arranged a banquet for the Lord and his Mother, and for all of His company. Among those that were at table with Them was Lazarus, whom He had brought back to life a few days before.

viii. Palm Sunday

On the morning of Palm Sunday, Jesus proceeded with His disciples toward Jerusalem, being accompanied by many angels, who sang hymns of praise at seeing Him so enamored of men and so solicitous for their eternal salvation. Having walked more or less of two miles and arrived in the village of Bethphage, He sent two disciples to an influential man of that neighborhood. From him they brought two beasts of burden, one of which had not yet been used or ridden by any one. The Lord progressed on his way to Jerusalem while they spread some of their cloaks and other garments both upon the ass and her colt. The Lord was to make use of both of them according to the prophecies of Isaias (Is.62, 11), and Zacharias (Zach. 9, 9), who had foretold these particulars many ages before, in order that the priests and scribes should not be able to allege ignorance as an excuse. All the four Evangelists describe this wonderful triumph of Christ and relate what was seen by the bodily eyes of those present. As they proceeded on their way the disciples, and with them all the people, the infants as well as the grown persons, hailed Jesus as the true Messiah, the Son of David, the Savior of the world and as their legitimate King.

Some of them exclaimed: "Peace be in heaven and glory in the highest, blessed be He that cometh as the King in the name of the Lord." Others, "Hosanna to the Son of David, save us, Son of David, blessed be the kingdom which now has arrived, the kingdom of our forefather David." Some others lopped branches from palms and other trees in signs triumph and joy, and spread their garments upon the ground to prepare a way for Jesus the triumphant Conqueror.

All these demonstrations of worship and admiration, which these men gave to Jesus the Incarnate Word, were to manifest the power of His Divinity, especially at this time, when the priests and pharisees were watching Him and seeking to put an end to His life in that very city. For if they had not been moved interiorly by a divine power, above and beyond that of their admiration for the miracles wrought by Him, it would have been impossible to draw such a gathering.

16. Holy Thursday

The Apostles asked Him where He wished to celebrate the Passover supper (Matt. 26); for on that Thursday night the Jews were to partake of the lamb of the Passover, a most notable and solemn national feast. Though of all their feasts, this eating of the paschal lamb was most prophetic and significant of the Messiah and of the mysteries connected with Him and His work, the Apostles were as yet scarcely aware of its intimate connection with Jesus. Jesus answered by sending St. Peter and St. John to Jerusalem to make arrangements for the Passover supper. This was to be in a house, where they would see a servant enter with a jug of water, and whose master they were to request in Jesus' name to prepare a room for His Last Supper with His disciples. This man lived near Jerusalem; rich and influential, he was at the same time devoted to Jesus and was one of those who had witnessed and had believed in His miracles and teachings. Jesus rewarded his piety and devotion by choosing his house for the celebration of the great mystery, and thus consecrate it as a temple for the faithful of future times. The two Apostles immediately departed on their mission following their instructions, they asked the owner of this house to entertain the Master for the solemn celebration of this feast of the unleavened bread. The owner of what history refers to as "the upper room" was enlightened by special grace and he readily offered his dwelling with all the necessary furniture for celebrating the supper according to the law. He provided them a very large hall, appropriately tapestried and adorned for the mysteries which, unbeknown to him and the Apostles, the Lord Jesus would celebrate there. After due preparation had thus been made Jesus and the other Apostles arrived at this apartment. The Blessed Virgin Mary and the holy women in her company with the disciples came soon after.

Jesus, with his Apostles and disciples, took their places to celebrate the feast of the Passover lamb. After washing the feet of His Apostles and finishing their supper,

Jesus our Lord took into His venerable hands the bread, which lay upon the plate, and interiorly asked the permission and co-operation of the Eternal Father, that now and ever afterwards in virtue of the words about to be uttered by Him, and later to be repeated in His Holy Church, He should really and truly become present in the host, Himself to yield obedience to these sacred words. While making this petition He raised his eyes toward heaven with an expression of such sublime majesty, that He inspired the Apostles, the angels and His Blessed Mother with new and deepest reverence. Then He pronounced the words of consecration over the bread, changing its substance into the substance of His true body and immediately thereupon He uttered the words of consecration also over the wine, changing it into His true blood. As an answer to these words of consecration was heard the voice of the Eternal Father, saying: "This is my beloved Son, in whom I delight, and shall take my delight to the end of the world; and He shall be with men during all the time of their banishment." In like manner was this confirmed by the Holy Spirit. The most sacred humanity of Jesus, in the Person of the Word, gave tokens of profoundest veneration to the Divinity contained in the Sacrament of His body and blood. The Blessed Mother, in her retreat, prostrated herself on the ground and adored her Son in the blessed Sacrament with incomparable reverence. Then also the angels of her guard, all the angels of heaven, and among them likewise the souls of Enoch and Elias, in their own name and in the name of the holy Patriarchs and Prophets of the old law, fell down in adoration of their Lord God in the Holy Sacrament.

All the Apostles and disciples, who, with the exception of Judas the traitor, believed in this Holy Sacrament, adored it with great humility and reverence according to each one's disposition. The great high priest Jesus Christ raised up His own consecrated body and blood in order that all who were present at this first Mass might adore it in a special manner. During this elevation His most pure Mother, St. John, Enoch and Elias, were favored with an special insight into the mystery of His presence in the sacred species.

They understood more profoundly, how, in the species of the bread, was contained His body and in those of the wine, His blood; how in both, on account of the inseparable union of His soul with His body and blood, was present the living and true Christ; how with the Person of the Word, was also therein united the Person of the Father and of the Holy Spirit; and how therefore, on account of the inseparable existence and union of the Father, Son and Holy Spirit, the Holy Eucharist contained the perfect humanity of Jesus the Lord with the three Divine Persons of the Godhead. Thus the Most High God is entirely present in the Holy Eucharist. All this was understood most profoundly by the Blessed Virgin Mary and by the others according to their degree. They understood also the efficacy of the words of the consecration, now endowed with such divine virtue, that as soon as they are pronounced with the intention of doing what Jesus did at that time, by any priest since that time over the proper material, they would change the bread into His body and the wine into His blood.

From the beginning of man until the institution of the Holy Eucharist, all of the angels felt and had great empathy for their inferior human beings. But at this special moment, the angels felt lacking because they did not have a physical body to be able to receive, hold and contain the physical presence and entire God, as the Father, Son and Holy Spirit. And henceforth, the Angels would no longer think of mankind as inferior creatures.

17. Passion of Jesus

[Editor's note: For brevity, much of the information that is described in the Gospels has been deliberately omitted herein.]

i. Jesus' Agony in the Garden

Jesus left the house of the Cenacle (the upper room) with all the men who had been present at His Last Supper; and many of them dispersed in the different streets in order to attend to their own affairs. Followed by His twelve Apostles, the Lord Jesus directed His steps toward the Mount of Olives outside and close to the eastern walls of Jerusalem. Judas conjectured that Jesus intended to pass the night in prayer as was His custom; this presented the opportune occasion for delivering Jesus into the hands of His enemies, the scribes and the pharisees. Thus, Judas lagged behind while Jesus and His Apostles went on. He departed in all haste and arrived breathless at the house of the high priests. On his way, Lucifer perceiving the haste of Judas in procuring the death of Jesus, and fearing that Jesus might be the true Messiah, came toward him in the shape of a very wicked man, a friend of Judas acquainted with the intended betrayal. In this shape Lucifer could speak to Judas without being recognized. He tried to persuade him that this project of selling his Master did at first seem advisable on account of the wicked deeds attributed to Jesus; but that, having more maturely considered the matter, he did not now deem it advisable to deliver Him over to the priests and pharisees; for Jesus was not so bad as Judas might imagine; nor did He deserve death; and besides He might free Himself by some miracles and involve his betrayer into great difficulties.

Thus Lucifer, seized by new fear, sought to counteract the suggestions with which he had previously filled the heart of the perfidious disciple against Jesus. He hoped to confuse his victim; but his new villainy was in vain. For Judas, having voluntarily lost his faith and not being troubled by any such strong suspicions as Lucifer, preferred to take his Master's life rather than to encounter the wrath of the pharisees for permitting him to live unmolested.

Filled with this fear and his abominable avarice, he took no account of the counsel of Lucifer, although he had no suspicion of his not being the friend, whose shape the devil had assumed. Being stripped of grace he neither desired, nor could be persuaded by anyone to turn back in his malice. The priests, having heard that Jesus was in Jerusalem, had gathered to consult about the promised betrayal. Judas entered and told them that he had left his Master with the other disciples on their way to the Mount of Olives; that this seemed to be the most favorable occasion for His arrest, since on this night they had already made sufficient preparation and taken enough precaution to prevent His escaping their hands.

Jesus pursued His way across the torrent of Cedron (John 18, 1) to the Mount of Olives and entered the Garden of Gethsemane. Then He said to all the Apostles: "Wait for Me, and seat yourselves here while I go a short distance from here to pray (Matt. 26, 36), do you also pray in order that you may not enter into temptation" (Luke 22, 40). Then Jesus leaving the band of eight Apostles at that place and taking with Him St. Peter, St. John, and St. James, retired to another place, where they could neither be seen nor heard by the rest (Mark 14, 33). Being with the three Apostles He raised his eyes up to the Eternal Father confessing and praising Him as was His custom. In this prayer Jesus Christ our Lord offered Himself anew to the Eternal Father in satisfaction of His justice for the rescue of the human race; and He gave consent, that all the torments of His Passion and Death be let loose over that part of His human being, which was capable of suffering. From that moment He suspended and restrained whatever consolation or relief would otherwise overflow from the impassible to the passible part of his being, so that in this dereliction his passion and sufferings might reach the highest degree possible. The Eternal Father granted these petitions and approved this total sacrifice of the sacred humanity.

Jesus said to Peter, James and John: "Wait for Me, watch and pray with Me." With this exhortation the Lord Jesus separated Himself a short distance from the three Apostles. He threw himself upon the ground and prayed to the Eternal Father: "Father, if it is possible, let this chalice pass from Me" (Matt. 26, 38).

107

At this moment, Jesus discussed the most important matter of all with the Eternal Father, namely, how far the Redemption gained by His Passion and Death should affect the number of souls to be saved. In this prayer Christ offered, on his part, to the Eternal Father His torments, His precious blood and His Death for all men as an abundant and more than equitable price for all the mortals and for each one of the human beings born till that time and yet to be born to the end of the world; and, on the part of mankind, He presented the infidelity, ingratitude and contempt with which sinful man was to respond to his frightful Passion and Death; He presented also the loss which He was to sustain from those who would not profit by his clemency and condemn themselves to eternal woe. Though to die for his friends and for the predestined was pleasing to Him and longingly desired by our Savior; yet to die for the reprobate was indeed bitter and painful; for with regard to them the impelling motive for accepting the pains of death was wanting. This sorrow was what the Lord called a chalice, for the Hebrews were accustomed to use this word for signifying anything that implied great labor and pain. Jesus requested that His Father let this chalice of dying for the reprobate pass from Him. Since now His Death was not to be evaded, He asked that none should be lost; He pleaded, that His Redemption would be enough for all, that therefore it should be applied to all in such a way as to make all, if possible, enter into heaven for all eternity.

Jesus knew His sufferings and death would be the most painful and intensely horrific that anyone would ever suffer. These physical sufferings which He knew from the beginning of His Incarnation, Jesus gladly accepted and was willing to endure many times over for the salvation of man. Jesus' greatest torment that caused Him the most anxiety, prompted Him to say: "My soul is sorrowful even unto death." And that made Him sweat blood in the Garden. And that ultimately led to the Eternal Father's decision against Him causing Jesus to say: "My God, My God why have You forsaken Me." All occurred over the only disagreement that ever happened between God the Father and His Onlybegotten Son which began in the Garden after His Last Supper and concluded when He died on the cross.

The argument began with Jesus proposing to His Eternal Father that just as all mankind was condemned by the sin of one man Adam that it was justified that His suffering and death of one man Himself should redeem all mankind. Jesus' rational and logical argument was equitable and sensible. But the Eternal Father's perspective was very different. God the Father wanted only those persons that would not only accept Jesus as their Lord and Savior but would live according to His example and teachings. The Blessed Virgin Mary was agreeable with Jesus' proposal and saw the equity and justification of both positions. Jesus would lose His argument as the Eternal Father's Will shall always prevail. Because of this, the Blessed Virgin Mary says that the majority of souls of mankind will be forever condemned. As one third of the angels were damned then more than fifty-one percent of the entire human race will be damned.

ii. Judas betrays Jesus

At the instigation of Judas they hastily gathered together a large band of people, composed of pagan soldiers, a tribune, and many Jews. Having consigned to them Judas as a hostage, they sent this band on its way to apprehend Jesus, who was awaiting them and who was aware of all the thoughts and schemes. All these servants carried weapons, ropes and chains. With torches and lanterns they went from the city to the Mount of Olives. Judas was the leader of these servants and insisted upon much precaution as he feared that Jesus, whom he believed to be a magician and sorcerer, would perform some miracle for His escape. As if men with swords and clubs could have ever conquered the Lord Jesus should He have decided to make use of His divine power!

While Judas and his band were approaching, Jesus returned the third time to his Apostles and finding them asleep spoke to them: "Sleep ye now, and take your rest. It is enough, the hour is come. Behold the Son of man shall be betrayed into the hands of sinners. Rise up, let us go. Behold he that will betray Me is at hand." (Mark 14, 41). Such were the words of Jesus to Peter, James and John. Being sad and fatigued they did not know how to answer Jesus. They arose and went with Jesus to join the other eight Apostles.

During these words and prayers of Jesus, Judas advanced in order to give Jesus a kiss to signal for the soldiers to take Jesus prisoner. Then Jesus said to them: "Whom do you seek?" and they answered Him: "Jesus of Nazareth." As the Lord spoke with divine power, His enemies could not resist and at His words, they all fell backwards to the ground. This happened not only to the soldiers, but to the dogs, which they had brought with them, and to the horses on which some of them rode: all of them fell to the ground and remained motionless like stones. Lucifer and his demons were hurled down with them, deprived of motion and suffering new confusion and torture. They all remained for some seven or eight minutes, showing no more signs of life than if they had died.

A second time Jesus said to them: "Whom do you seek?" and they again answered: "Jesus of Nazareth." The Lord Jesus answered most meekly: "I have already told you, that I am He. If it is Me that you want, let these others go their way." (John 18, 8). By this statement Jesus gave permission to that whole miserable band of men, demons and animals to arise and be restored to the same condition as before their falling down. With these words He gave permission to the servants and the soldiers to take Him prisoner and execute their designs.
The first one who quickly approached in order to lay hands upon Jesus, was a servant of the high priest named Malchus. In spite of the fear and consternation of all the Apostles, St. Peter, more than all the rest, was roused with zeal for the defense of the honor and life of the Lord Jesus. Drawing a sword which he had with him, he slashed at Malchus and cut off one of his ears, severing it entirely from the head (John 18, 10). The stroke would have resulted in a much more serious wound, if it were not for Jesus' healing power. Jesus picked up the severed ear and restored it to its place, perfectly healing the wound and making Malchus more sound and whole than he was before. But He first turned to St. Peter and reprehended him, saying: "Put up thy sword into the scabbard, for all that shall take it to kill with it, shall perish. Do thou not wish that I drink the chalice, which My Father hath given Me? Think thou that I cannot ask my Father, and He will give me presently five thousand legions of angels for My defense? But how then shall the Scriptures and the Prophets be fulfilled?" (John 18, 11; Matt. 26, 53).

Then Christ our Lord, turning toward his enemies and the servants of the Jews, spoke to them with great majesty and grandeur: "You are come as it were to a robber with swords and clubs to apprehend Me. I sat daily with you, teaching in the temple, and you laid not hands on Me. But this is your hour and the power of darkness." (Matt. 26, 55; Luke 22, 53).

Then they fiercely seized Jesus, binding Him securely with ropes and chains. Jesus was dragged from the garden to the house of the highpriests, first to the house of Annas (John 18, 13). The turbulent band of soldiers and servants, having been advised by Judas that his Master was a sorcerer and could easily escape their hands, if they did not carefully bind and chain Him securely before starting on their way, took all precautions inspired by such a mistrust (Mark 14, 44). Lucifer and his demons secretly irritated and provoked them to increase their ill-treatment of the Lord Jesus beyond all bounds of humanity and decency. As they were willing accomplices of Lucifer's malice, they omitted no outrage against the person of their Creator within the limits set them by the Almighty. They bound Him with a heavy iron chain with such ingenuity, that it encircled as well the waist as the neck. The two ends of the chain, which remained free, were attached to large rings or handcuffs, with which they shackled the hands of the Lord, who created the heavens, the angels and the whole universe. The hands thus secured and bound, they fastened not in front, but behind. This chain they had brought from the house of Annas the highpriest, where it had served to raise the portcullis of a dungeon. They had wrenched it from its place and provided it with padlock handcuffs. But they were not satisfied with this unheard-of way of securing a prisoner; for in their distrust they added two pieces of strong rope: the one they wound around the throat of Jesus and, crossing it at the breast, bound it in heavy knots all about the body, leaving two long ends free in front, in order that the servants and soldiers might jerk Him in different directions along the way. The second rope served to tie his arms, being bound likewise around his waist. The two ends of this rope were left hanging free to be used by two other executioners for jerking Him from behind.

Some of them dragged Him along by the ropes in front and others retarded his steps by the ropes hanging from the handcuffs behind. In this manner, with a violence unheard of, they sometimes forced Him to run forward in haste, frequently causing Him to fall; at others they jerked Him backwards; and then again they pulled Him from one side to the other, according to their diabolical whims. Many times they violently threw Him to the ground and as his hands were tied behind He fell upon it with his divine countenance and was severely wounded and lacerated. In His falls they pounced upon Him, inflicting blows and kicks, trampling upon his body and upon his head and face. All these deviltries they accompanied with festive shouts and degrading insults.

Lucifer roused in Judas a keen sorrow for his misdeeds; not however for a good purpose, nor founded upon having offended the divine Truth, but upon his disgrace among men and upon the fear of retribution from his Master, whom he knew to be miraculously powerful and One whom he would be able to escape nowhere in the whole world. Everywhere the blood of the just One would forever cry for vengeance against him. Filled with these thoughts and others aroused by the demon, he was involved in confusion, darkness and rabid rage against himself. Fleeing from all human beings he essayed to throw himself from the highest roof of the priests house without being able to execute his design. Gnawing like a wild beast at the flesh of his arms and hands, striking fearful blows at his head, tearing out his hair and raving in his talk, he rushed away and showered maledictions and execrations upon himself as the most unfortunate and miserable of men. Seeing him thus beside himself Lucifer inspired him with the thought of hunting up the priests, returning to them the money and confessing his sin. This Judas hastened to do, and he loudly shouted at them those words: "I have sinned, betraying innocent blood!" (Matt. 27, 4). But they, not less hardened, answered that he should have seen to that before. The intention of the demon was to hinder the death of Christ if possible. This repulse of the priests, so full of impious cruelty, took away all hope from Judas and he persuaded himself that it was impossible to hinder the death of his Master. So thought also the demon, although later on he made more efforts to forestall it through Pilate.

But as Judas could be of no more use to him for his purpose, he augmented his distress and despair, persuading him that in order to avoid severer punishments he must end his life. Judas yielded to this terrible deceit, and rushing forth from the city, hung himself on a dried-out fig tree (Matt. 27, 5). Thus he that was the murderer of his Creator, became also his own murderer. This happened on Friday at twelve o clock, three hours before our Savior died.

The demons at once took possession of the soul of Judas and brought it down to hell. His entrails burst from the body hanging upon the tree (Acts 1, 18). All that saw this stupendous punishment of the perfidious and malicious disciple for his treason, were filled with astonishment and dread. The body remained hanging by the neck for three days, exposed to the view of the public. During that time the Jews attempted to take it down from the tree and to bury it in secret, for it was a sight apt to cause great confusion to the pharisees and priests, who could not refute such a testimony of his wickedness. But no efforts of theirs sufficed to drag or separate the body from its position on the tree until three days had passed, when the demons themselves snatched the body from the tree and brought it to his soul, in order that both might suffer eternal punishment in the deepest abyss of hell. Among the obscure caverns of the infernal prisons was a very large one, arranged for more horrible chastisements than the others, and which was still unoccupied; for the demons had been unable to cast any soul into it, although their cruelty had induced them to attempt it many times from the time of Cain unto that day. All hell had remained astonished at the failure of these attempts, being entirely ignorant of the mystery, until the arrival of the soul of Judas, which they readily succeeded in hurling and burying in this prison never before occupied by any of the damned. The secret of it was, that this cavern of greater torments and fiercer fires of hell, from the creation of the world, had been destined for those, who, after having received Baptism, would damn themselves by the neglect of the Sacraments, the doctrines, the Passion and Death of Jesus the Savior, and the intercession of His Blessed Mother.

iii. Jesus is taken to the highpriests

Before the high priest Annas, Jesus was silent and opened not his mouth, as Isaias prophesied (53, 7). Imperiously and haughtily the high priest asked Him about His disciples (John 18, 19), and what doctrine He was preaching and teaching. Jesus answered the question as to His doctrines: "I have spoken openly to everyone. I have always taught in the synagogue and in the temple, whither all the Jews resort and in secret I have spoken nothing. Why ask thou Me? ask those, who have heard what I have spoken unto them: behold they know what I have said." Concerning the Apostles Jesus said nothing. One of the servants of the high priest rushed up with raised hand and audaciously struck the venerable and sacred face of Jesus, saying: "Answer Thou the high priest so?" The Lord accepted this boundless injury, praying for the one who had inflicted it; and holding Himself ready, if necessary, to turn and offer the other cheek for a second stroke, according to the doctrine He had himself inculcated (Matt. 5, 39). But in order that the atrocious and daring offender might not shamelessly boast of his wickedness, the Lord replied with great tranquility and meekness: "If I have spoken evil, give testimony of the evil; if well, why strike thou Me?"

While this ill-treatment of Jesus was going on, St. Peter and the other disciple, who was none other than St. John, arrived at the house of Annas. St. John, as being well known there, readily obtained entrance, while St. Peter remained outside. Afterwards the servant maid, who was an acquaintance of St. John, allowed also him to enter and see what would happen to Jesus (John 18, 16). The two disciples remained in the portico adjoining the court-hall of the priest, and St. Peter approached the fire, which the soldiers, on account of the coldness of the night, had built in the enclosure near the portico. The servant maid, on closer inspection, noticed the depressed bearing of saint Peter. Coming up to him she recognized him as a disciple of Jesus, and said: "Art thou not perhaps one of the disciples of this Man?" Peter answered: "I am not his disciple." Having given this answer, he slipped away to avoid further conversation, and left the premises. But he soon afterwards followed Jesus to the house of Caiphas, where he denied Him again at two different times.

The denial of Peter caused greater pain to Jesus than the beating which He had received; for this sin was directly opposed and abhorrent to His immense charity, while pains and sufferings were welcome to Him, since He could thereby atone for our sins. After this first denial of Peter, Jesus prayed for him to His Eternal Father and ordained that through the intercession of the Blessed Virgin Mary, Peter would obtain pardon even after his third denial.

iv. Jesus is dragged to the house of Caiphas

After Jesus had been thus insulted and struck in the house of Annas, He was sent, bound and fettered as He was, to the priest Caiphas, the father-in-law of Annas, who in that year officiated as the prince and high priest; with him were gathered the scribes and distinguished men of the Jews in order to urge the condemnation of Jesus.

The highpriest Caiphas, filled with envy and hatred against Jesus, was seated in his chair of state or throne. With him were Lucifer and all his demons, who had come from the house of Annas. The scribes and pharisees surrounded Jesus. By common consent they sought for witnesses, whom they could bribe to bring false testimonies against Jesus our Savior (Matt. 26, 59). Those that had been procured, advanced to proffer their accusations and testimony; but their accusations neither agreed with each other, nor could any of their slander be made to apply to Him, who of his very nature was innocence and holiness (Mark 25, 56; Heb. 7, 26). In order not to be foiled, they brought two other false witnesses, who deposed, that they had heard Jesus say, He could destroy the temple of God made by the hands of men, and build up another one in three days, not made by them (Mark 16, 58). This testimony did not seem to be of much value, although they founded upon it the accusation, that He attributed to Himself divine power. Even if this testimony had not been false in itself, the saying, if uttered by the Lord Almighty, would have been infallibly true and could not have been presumptuous or false. But the testimony was false; since the Lord had not uttered these words in reference to the material temple of God, as the witnesses wished to inculcate.

At the time when He expelled the buyers and sellers from the temple and when asked by what power He did it, He answered: "Destroy this temple" that is: destroy this sacred human , and on the third day I shall restore it, which He certainly did at his Resurrection in testimony of his divine power.

Jesus remained silent to Caiphas' accusations. Caiphas, provoked by the patient silence of Jesus, rose up in his seat and said to Him: "Why dost Thou not answer to what so many witnesses testify against Thee?" But even to this Jesus made no response.

Lucifer stirred up Caiphas to the highest pitch of rage to ask in great wrath and haughtiness: "I adjure Thee by the living God, that Thou tell us, if Thou be the Christ, the Son of God." Out of reverence for the name of God Jesus answered: "Thou hast said: I am He. Nevertheless, I say to you, hereafter you shall see the Son of man (who I am) sitting on the right hand of the power of God, and coming in the clouds of heaven" (Matt. 26, 64). At this divine answer the demons and the men were affected in different ways. Lucifer and his devils could not bear it; but immediately felt a superior force, which hurled them down into the abyss and oppressed them by the truth it contained. And they would not have dared to come again into the presence of Christ our Savior, if the divine Providence had not allowed them to fall again into doubts, whether this Man Christ had really spoken the truth or had merely sought this means of freeing Himself from the hands of the Jews. This uncertainty gave them new courage and they came forth once more to the battlefield. The ultimate triumph over the demons was reserved to the Cross itself, on which the Savior was to vanquish both them and death, as Zachary had prophesied and as will appear later.

But the high priest, furious at the answer of the Lord, instead of looking upon it as a solution of his doubt, rose once more in his seat, and tearing his garments as an outward manifestation of his zeal for the honor of God, loudly cried out: "He hath blasphemed; what further need have we of witnesses? Behold, now you have heard the blasphemy: what do you think?" (Matt. 26, 65.)

All exclaimed in a loud voice: "He is guilty of death (Matt. 26, 66), let Him die, let Him die!" They covered his face and then struck Him with their hands and fists saying: "Prophesy, prophesy to us, Thou Prophet, who was it that struck Thee?" Some of them struck Him in the face, others kicked Him, others tore out his hair, others spat upon his face.

Peter followed Jesus from the house of Annas to the house of Caiphas. Among the great multitude which crowded in and out of the house of Caiphas and in the darkness, it was not difficult for Peter to find entrance into the house of Caiphas. In the gates of the courtyard a servant-maid, who was a portress as in the house of Annas, likewise noticed saint Peter; she immediately went up to the soldiers, who stood at the fire with him and said: "This man is one of those who were wont to accompany Jesus of Nazareth." One of the bystanders said: "Thou art surely a Galilean and one of them." Saint Peter denied it and added an oath, that he was not a disciple of Jesus, immediately leaving the company at the fire. Yet, in his eagerness to see the end, although he left the courtyard, he did not leave the neighborhood. His natural love and compassion for the Lord still caused him to linger in the place, where he saw Him suffer so much. So the Apostle moved about, sometimes nearer, sometimes farther from the hall of justice for nearly an hour. Then a relative of that Malchus, whose ear Peter had severed, recognized him and said: Thou art a Galilean and a disciple of Jesus; I saw thee with Him in the garden." Then Peter deeming himself discovered, was seized with still greater fear, and he began to assert with oaths and imprecations, that he knew not the Man (Matt. 26, 72). Immediately thereupon the cock crowed the second time, and the prediction of his divine Master, that he should deny Him thrice before the cock crowed twice, was fulfilled to the letter.
...
By the ill-treatment, which the Lord received in the presence of Caiphas, the wrath of this high priest and of all his supporters and ministers was much gratified, though not at all satiated. But as it was already past midnight, the whole council of these wicked men resolved to take good care, that the Savior be securely watched and confined until the morning, lest He should escape while they were asleep.

For this purpose they ordered Him to be locked, bound as He was, in one of the subterranean dungeons, a prison cell set apart for the most audacious robbers and criminals of the state. Scarcely any light penetrated into this prison to dispel its darkness. It was filled with such uncleanness and stench, that it would have infected the whole house, if it had not been so remote and so well enclosed; for it had not been cleaned for many years, both because it was so deep down and because of the degradation of the criminals that were confined in it; for none thought it worthwhile making it more habitable than for mere wild beasts, unworthy of all human kindness.

The order of the council of wickedness was executed; the servants dragged the Creator of heaven and earth to that polluted and subterranean dungeon there to imprison Him. As the Lord was still bound with the fetters laid upon Him in the garden, these malicious men freely exercised all the wrathful cruelty with which they were inspired by the prince of darkness; for they dragged Him forward by the ropes, inhumanly causing Him to stumble, and loading Him with kicks and cuffs amid blasphemous imprecations. From the floor in one corner of the subterranean cavern protruded part of a rock or block, which on account of its hardness had not been cut out. To this block, which had the appearance of a piece of column, they now bound and fettered the Lord Jesus with the ends of the ropes, but in a most merciless manner. For they forced Him to approach it and tied Him to it in a stooping position, so that He could neither seat Himself nor stand upright for relief, forcing Him to remain in a most painful and torturing posture. Thus they left Him bound to the rock, closing the prison-door with a key and giving it in charge of one of the most malicious of their number.

Some time later, torturers of the high priest entered into the dungeon cell and removed Jesus from the stone block and placed Him in the middle of the dungeon, at the same time blindfolding Him with a cloth; there they began to come up one after the other and strike Him with their fists, or slap or kick Him, each one trying to outdo the other in vehemence of their blasphemous cruelty and asking Him to prophesy who had struck Him.

118

Lucifer, tormented by his anxious desire of seeing some sign of impatience in Jesus lashed into fury at the equanimity with which the Savior bore it all. Therefore, he inspired those slaves and friends of his with the project of despoiling the Lord of all his clothes and pursuing their ill-treatment according to suggestions which could only originate in the execrable demon. They readily yielded to this new inspiration and set about to afflict the Lord Jesus.

Then they dragged Jesus up to the council of Caiphas. Jesus did not speak; but the tortures, the blows and the spittle, with which they had covered Him and which He could not wipe off on account of his bonds, had so disfigured Him, that the members of the council were dreadfully surprised at Jesus' appearance.

They again asked Him to tell them, whether He was the Christ (Luke 22, 1), that is, the Anointed. Just as all their previous questions, so this was put with the malicious determination not to listen or to admit the truth, but to calumniate and fabricate a charge against Him.

He therefore said to them: "If I tell you that I am He of whom you ask, you will not believe what I say; and if I shall ask you, you will not answer, nor release Me. But I tell you, that the Son of man, after this, shall seat Himself at the right hand of the power of God" (Luke 22, 67). The priests answered: "Then thou art the Son of God?" and the Lord replied: "You say that I am." … … …

v. Jesus is taken to Pilate

The high priest torturers brought Jesus to the house of Pilate still bound with the same chains and ropes in which they had taken Him from the garden. The city of Jerusalem was full of strangers, who had come from all Israel to celebrate the great Passover with the feast of the Lamb and of the unleavened bread. As the rumor of this arrest was already spread among the people, Jesus was known to all of them, a countless multitude gathered in the streets to see Him brought in chains through the streets.

They were divided in their opinion concerning the Messiah; some of them shouted out: "Let Him die, let Him die, this wicked impostor, who deceives the whole world." Others answered: His doctrines do not appear to be so bad, nor his works; for He has done good to many. Still others, who had believed in Him, were much afflicted and wept; while the whole city was in confusion and uproar concerning Jesus of Nazareth.

Lucifer could not understand how Jesus allowing Himself to be despised, ill-treated and permit so much bodily harm to Himself could never harmonize with His being true God; for, if He were God, said Lucifer to himself, His Divinity would never consent to such annihilation.

Pilate, although a heathen, yielded to their ceremonious scruples, and seeing that they hesitated to enter his pretorium, he went out to meet them. According to the formality customary among the Romans, he asked them (John 18, 28): "What accusation have you against this Man?" They answered: "If He were not a criminal, we would not have brought Him to thee thus bound and fettered." This was as much as to say: We have convinced ourselves of his misdeeds and we are so attached to justice and to our obligations, that we would not have begun any proceedings against Him, if He were not a great malefactor. But Pilate pressed his inquiry and said: "What then are the misdeeds, of which He has made Himself guilty?" They answered: "He is convicted of disturbing the commonwealth, He wishes to make Himself our king and forbids paying tribute to Caesar (Luke 23, 2) ; He claims to be the son of God, and has preached a new doctrine, commencing in Galilee, through all Judea and Jerusalem." Then Pilate said to them: "Take Him then yourselves and judge Him according to your laws; I do not find a just cause for proceeding against Him." But the Jews replied: "It is not permitted us to sentence any one to death, nor to execute such a sentence."

Pilate asked Jesus: "How do You answer to the accusations which they bring against Thee?" But the Savior answered not one word in the presence of his accusers, causing much wonder in Pilate at such silence and patience. But, desiring to inquire more closely, whether Jesus was truly a King, he withdrew from the clamoring Jews and brought Jesus into the pretorium. There he asked Him face to face: "Tell me, can it be that Thou art a King of the Jews?" Pilate could not bring himself to think that He was a King in fact; since he knew that Christ was not reigning. Therefore, he wished to find out, whether Jesus claimed or really possessed any right to the title of King. Our Savior answered him: "Say thou this thing of thyself, or have others told it thee of Me?" (John 18, 34). Pilate replied: "Am I a Jew? Thy own nation and the chief priests have delivered Thee up to me. What hast Thou done?" Jesus answered: "My kingdom is not of this world. If my kingdom were of this world, my servants would certainly strive that I be not delivered to the Jews: but now my kingdom is not here." Pilate answered: "Art Thou a king then?" Jesus answered: "Thou say that I am a king. For this I was born and for this I came into the world. Every one that is of the Truth, hears my voice." Pilate wondered at this answer and asked: "What is truth?" But without waiting for an answer, he left Him in the pretorium, and said to the Jews: "I find no cause in Him. But you have a custom, that I should release one unto you at the Passover, will you, therefore, that I release unto you the King of the Jews, or Barabbas?"

This Barabbas was a thief and murderer, who had killed someone in a quarrel. All the people raised their voice and said: "We desire that you release Barabbas, and crucify Jesus." In this demand they persisted until it was granted.

vi. Pilate sends Jesus to Herod

One of the accusations of the Jews and the priests before Pilate was, that Jesus our Savior had begun to stir up the people by his preaching in the province of Galilee (Luke 23, 6). This caused Pilate to inquire, whether He was a Galilean; and as they told him, that Jesus was born and raised in that country, he thought this circumstance useful for the solution of his difficulties in regard to Jesus and for escaping the molestations of the Jews, who so urgently demanded his death. Herod was at that time in Jerusalem, celebrating the Pasch of the Jews. He was the son of the first Herod, who had murdered the Innocents to procure the death of Jesus soon after his birth (Matt. 2, 16). This murderer had become a proselyte of the Jews at the time of his marriage with a Jewish woman. On this account his son Herod likewise observed the law of Moses, and he had come to Jerusalem from Galilee, of which he was governor. Pilate was at enmity with Herod, for the two governed the two principal provinces of Israel namely, Judea and Galilee, and a short time before it had happened that Pilate, in his zeal for the supremacy of the Roman empire, had murdered some Galileans during a public function in the temple, mixing the blood of the insurgents with that of the holy sacrifices. Herod was highly incensed at this sacrilege, and Pilate, in order to afford him some satisfaction without much trouble to himself, resolved to send to him Jesus to be examined and judged as one of the subjects of Herod's sway. Pilate also expected that Herod would set Jesus free as being innocent and a Victim of the malice and envy of the priests and scribes.

Jesus was then dragged from the house of Pilate to the palace of Herod, being still bound and chained as before and accompanied by the scribes and priests as his accusers. There were also a large number of soldiers and servants, who dragged Him along by the ropes and cleared the streets, which had been filled with multitudes of people to see the spectacle. The military broke their way through the crowds; and as the servants and priests were thirsting so eagerly for the blood of the Savior and wished to shed it on this very day, they hastened with the Lord through the streets nearly on a run and with great tumult. Mary also set forth from the house of Pilate with her company in order to follow her sweetest Son Jesus and accompany Him on the way, which He was still to go until his death on the Cross. It would not have been possible for the Lady to follow her Beloved closely enough to be in his sight, if She had not ordered her holy angels to open a way for Her.

They made it possible for Her to be constantly near her Son, so that She could enjoy his presence, though that also brought with it only a fuller participation in all torments and sorrows. She obtained the fulfillment of all her wishes; for walking along through the streets near the Savior She saw and heard the insults of the servants, the blows they dealt Him, the reproaches of the people, expressed either as their own or repeated from hearsay.

When Herod was informed that Pilate would send Jesus of Nazareth to him, he was highly pleased. He knew that Jesus was a great friend of John the Baptist, whom he had ordered to be put to death (Mark 6, 27), and had heard many reports of his preaching. In vain and foolish curiosity, he harbored the desire of seeing Jesus do something new and extraordinary for his entertainment and wonder (Luke 23, 8). Jesus was dragged into the presence of the murderer Herod.

The nobles and priests of the Jews stood around, continually rehearsing the same accusations and charges which they had advanced in the presence of Pilate. But the Lord maintained silence also in regard to these calumnies, much to the disappointment of Herod. In his presence the Lord would not open his lips, neither in order to answer his questions, nor in order to refute the accusations. Herod was altogether unworthy of hearing the truth, this being his greatest punishment and the punishment most to be dreaded by all the princes and the powerful of this earth. Herod was much put out by the silence and meekness of our Savior and was much disappointed in his vain curiosity. But the unjust judge tried to hide his confusion by mocking and ridiculing the innocent Master with his whole cohort of soldiers and ordering him to be sent back to Pilate. Herod showed himself thankful to Pilate for the courtesy of sending Jesus of Nazareth to be judged before his tribunal. He informed Pilate, that he found no cause in Him, but held Him to be an ignorant man of no consequence whatever. By the secret judgments of divine Wisdom, Herod and Pilate were reconciled on that day and thenceforward remained friends.

vii. Herod sends Jesus back to Pilate

Conducted by many soldiers, both of Herod and Pilate, amid a still greater concourse, tumult, and excitement of the people, Jesus returned from Herod to Pilate.

Pilate was again faced with Jesus in his palace and was confronted again by the Jews to condemn Him to death on the cross. Convinced of the innocence of Jesus and of the envy of the Jews, he was much put out at Herod again referring the disagreeable decision to his own tribunal. Feeling himself obliged in his quality of judge to give this decision, he sought to placate the Jews in different ways. One of these was a private interview with some of the servants and friends of the high priests. He urged them to prevail upon their masters and friends, not any more to ask for the release of the malefactor Barabbas, but instead demand the release of our Redeemer; and to be satisfied with some punishment he was willing to administer before setting Him free. This measure Pilate had taken before they arrived a second time to press their demand for a sentence upon Jesus. The proposal to choose between freeing either Barabbas or Jesus was made to the Jews, not only once, but two or three times. The first time before sending Him to Herod and the second time after his return; this is related by the Evangelists with some variation, though not essentially contradicting truth (Matt. 27, 17). Pilate spoke to the Jews and said: "You have brought this Man before me, accusing Him of perverting the people by his doctrines; and having examined Him in your presence, I was not convinced of the truth of your accusations. And Herod, to whom I have sent Him. and before whom you repeated your accusations, refused to condemn Him to death. It will be sufficient to correct and chastise Him for the present, in order that He may amend. As I am to release some malefactor for the feast of the Pasch, I will release Jesus, if you will have Him freed, and punish Barabbas." But the multitude of the Jews, thus informed how much Pilate desired to set Jesus free, shouted with one voice: "Enough, enough, not Christ, but Barabbas deliver unto us."

124

While Pilate was thus disputing with the Jews in the pretorium, his wife, Procula, happened to hear of his doings and she sent him a message telling him: "What hast thou to do with this Man? Let him go free; for I warn thee that I have had this very day some visions in regard to Him!"

viii. Jesus is scourged

The torturers of Jesus attempted to subject his body to this shame of total nakedness, seeking to despoil Him of the cincture, which covered his loins, but in that they failed; because, on touching it, their arms became paralyzed and stiff, as had happened also in the house of Caiphas, when they attempted to take off his clothes. All the six of his tormentors separately made the attempt with the same result. Yet afterwards, these ministers of evil, in order to scourge Him with greater effect, raised some of the coverings; for so much the Lord permitted, but not that He should be uncovered and despoiled of his garments entirely. The miracle of their being hindered and paralyzed in their brutal attempts did not, however, move or soften the hearts of these human beasts; but in their diabolical insanity they attributed it all to the supposed sorcery and witchcraft of the Author of truth and life.

Thus the Lord stood uncovered in the presence of a great multitude and the six torturers bound Him brutally to one of the columns in order to chastise Him so much the more at their ease. Then, two and two at a time, they began to scourge Him with such inhuman cruelty, as was possible only in men possessed by Lucifer, as were these executioners. The first two scourged the innocent Savior with hard and thick cords, full of rough knots, and in their fury strained all the powers of their body to inflict the blows. This first scourging raised in the body of the Lord great welts and livid tumors, so that the sacred blood gathered beneath the skin and disfigured his entire body. The first two having at length desisted, the second pair continued the scourging in still greater emulation; with hardened leather thongs they leveled their strokes upon the places already sore and caused the discolored tumors to break open and shed forth the sacred blood until it bespattered and drenched the garments of the torturers, running down also in streams to the pavement.

125

Those two gave way to the third pair of scourgers, who commenced to beat the Lord with extremely tough rawhides, dried hard like osier twigs. They scourged Him still more cruelly, because they were wounding, not so much his virginal body, as cutting into the wounds already produced by the previous scourging. Besides they had been secretly incited to greater fury by the demons, who were filled with new rage at the patience of Christ.

As the veins of the sacred body had now been opened and His whole Person seemed but one continued wound, the third pair found no more room for new wounds. Their ceaseless blows inhumanly tore the immaculate and virginal flesh of Christ our Redeemer and scattered many pieces of it about the pavement; so much so that a large portion of the shoulder-bones were exposed and showed red through the flowing blood; in other places also the bones were laid bare larger than the palm of the hand. In order to wipe out entirely that beauty, which exceeded that of all other men (Ps. 44, 3), they beat Him in the face and in the feet and hands, thus leaving unwounded not a single spot in which they exerted their fury and wrath. His blood flowed to the ground, gathering here and there in great abundance. The scourging in the face, and in the hands and feet, was unspeakably painful, because these parts are so full of sensitive and delicate nerves. His face became so swollen and wounded that the blood and the swellings blinded Him. In addition to their blows the torturers spirted upon Jesus their disgusting spittle and loaded Him with insults. The exact number of blows dealt out to the Savior from head to foot was 5,115 from the scourging.

During the entire Passion of Jesus the Blessed Mother felt in her own body all the torments of her Son. This was true also of the scourging which she felt in all the parts of her body, in the same intensity as they were felt by Jesus in His body. She shed no blood except what flowed from her eyes with her tears, nor was she lacerated in her flesh; yet the bodily pains so changed and disfigured Her, that St. John and the holy women in her company failed to find in Her any resemblance of Herself. Besides the tortures of the body, She suffered ineffable sorrows of her soul.

The executioners unbound Jesus from the column, and with imperious and blasphemous presumption commanded Him immediately to put on his garment. But while they had scourged the most meek Master, one of his tormentors, instigated by the devil, had hidden his clothes out of sight, in order to prolong the nakedness and exposure of his divine Person for their derision and sport. This evil purpose suggested by the devil, was well known to the Mother of the Lord. She therefore, making use of her power as Queen, commanded Lucifer and all his demons to leave the neighborhood and immediately compelled they fled. She gave orders that the tunic be brought by the holy angels within reach of her most holy Son, so that He could again cover his sacred and lacerated body. All this was immediately attended to, although the sacrilegious executioners understood not the miracle, nor how it had been wrought; they attributed it all to the sorcery and magic of the demon. After this protracted nakedness our Savior had, they clothed Him in a much torn and soiled mantle of purple color.

ix. Crowning of thorns

They placed upon his sacred head a bonnet made of woven thorns, to serve Him as a crown (John 19, 2). This cap was woven of thorn branches and in such a manner that many of the hard and sharp thorns would penetrate into the skull, some of them to the ears and others to the eyes. Hence one of the greatest tortures suffered by the Lord was that of the crown of thorns.

Instead of a scepter they placed into his hands a reed. They also threw over His shoulders a violet colored mantle, something of the style of capes as such a garment belonged to the vesture of a king. Then all the soldiers, in the presence of the priests and pharisees, gathered around Him and heaped upon Him their blasphemous mockery and derision. Some of them bent their knees and mockingly said to Him: God save Thee, King of the Jews.

Others buffeted Him; others snatched the reed from his hands and struck Him on his crowned head; others ejected their disgusting spittle upon Him; all of them, instigated by Lucifer's furious demons, insulted and affronted Him in different manners.

The torturers returned Jesus to Pilate. And the crowd persisted in their request to crucify Jesus. Pilate answered: "Take Him yourselves and crucify Him, for I do not find any cause against Him." They replied: "According to our law He is guilty of death, for He claims to be the Son of God." This reply threw Pilate into greater consternation and he withdrew with Jesus into the pretorium, where speaking with Him alone, he asked Him where He came from. Jesus did not answer this question. Then Pilate said to Jesus "Do Thou then not speak to me? Do Thou not know, that I have power to crucify Thee and power to dismiss Thee?" Jesus answered: "Thou would not have any power over Me, unless it were given thee from above. Therefore, he that has delivered Me to thee, has the greater sin."

The priests became aware of Pilate's intentions to release Jesus and threatened him with the displeasure of the emperor, which he would incur, if he permitted this Jesus to go free. The pharisees said: "If thou free this Man, thou art no friend of Caesar; since he who makes a king of himself rises up against his orders and commands."

Pilate was much disturbed at this malicious and threatening intimation of the Jews, and seating himself in his tribunal at the sixth hour in order to pass sentence upon Jesus, he once more turned to plead with the Jews, saying: "See there your King!" And all of them answered: "Away with Him, away with Him, crucify Him!" He replied: "Shall I crucify your King?" where upon they shouted unanimously: "We have no other king than Caesar."

18. Crucifixion

Pilate seated in his tribunal pronounced the sentence of death against Jesus. All this was well known to the sorrowful Blessed Mother, who, though outside of the hall of judgment, saw all the proceedings by exalted vision.

Pilate's sentence of death decree for Jesus of Nazareth is lengthy and appears in its entirety in "Ciudad de Dios" Volume III Book Two Chapter XXI.

According to the reckoning in "Ciudad de Dios" the creation of the world happened in March; and from the day on which Adam was created until the Incarnation of the Word is 5199 years. Add the nine months, during which He remained in the virginal womb of his most holy Mother, and the thirty-three years of his life, we complete the 5233 years and three months, which according to the reckoning of the Romans intervened between the anniversary of His birth and the 25th of March, the day of His death.

After the sentence of Pilate against Jesus was published in a loud voice before all the people, the executioners loaded the heavy Cross, on which He was to be crucified, upon his tender and wounded shoulders. In order that He might carry it they loosened the bonds holding his hands, but not the others, since they wished to drag Him along by the loose ends of the ropes that bound his body. In order to torment Him the more they drew two loops around his throat. The Cross was fifteen feet long, of thick and heavy timbers. The herald began to proclaim the sentence and the whole confused and turbulent multitude of the people, the executioners and soldiers, with great noise, uproar and disorder began to move from the house of Pilate to mount Calvary through the streets of Jerusalem. The streets were full of shouting and clamoring people, but Jesus opened a passage to clear Himself a path to Calvary.

The executioners dragged Jesus along with incredible cruelty and insults. Some of them jerked Him forward by the ropes in order to accelerate his passage, while others pulled from behind in order to retard it. On account of this jerking and the weight of the Cross they caused Him to sway to and fro and often to fall to the ground. By the hard knocks He thus received on the rough stones great wounds were opened, especially on the two knees and they were widened at each repeated fall. The heavy Cross also inflicted a wound on the shoulder on which it was carried. The unsteadiness caused the Cross sometimes to knock against His head, and sometimes His head against the Cross; thus the thorns of His crown penetrated deeper and wounded the parts, which they had not yet reached. To these torments of the body the ministers of evil added many insulting words and affronts, ejecting their impure spittle and throwing the dirt of the pavement into his face so mercilessly, that they blinded the eyes that looked upon them with such divine mercy. By the haste with which they dragged Him along in their eagerness to see Him die, they did not allow Him to catch his breath; for his most innocent body, having been in so few hours overwhelmed with such a storm of torments, was so weakened and bruised, that to all appearances He was ready to yield up life under his pains and sorrows.

From the house of Pilate the sorrowful Blessed Mother followed with the multitudes on the way of her divine Son, accompanied by St. John and the pious women. As the surging crowds hindered Her from getting very near to Jesus, she asked the Eternal Father to be permitted to stand at the foot of the Cross of her blessed Son and see Him die with her own eyes. With the divine consent She ordered her holy angels to manage things in such a way as to make it possible for Her to execute her wishes. The holy angels obeyed her with great reverence; and they speedily led her through some bystreets in order that she might meet her Son. Thus it came that both of Them met face to face. Yet They did not speak to one another, nor would the fierce cruelty of the executioners have permitted such a conversation.

Simon, of Cyrene, the father of the disciples Alexander and Rufus, happened to come along. He was called by this name because he was a native of Cyrene, a city of Lybia, and had come to Jerusalem. This Simon was now forced by the Jews to carry the Cross a part of the way. The Cyrenean took hold of the Cross and Jesus was made to follow between the two thieves, in order that all might believe Him to be a criminal and malefactor like to them. The Blessed Mother walked very closely behind Jesus, as she desired and asked of the Eternal Father. To His divine will she conformed Herself in all the labors and torments of her Son, witnessing with her own eyes and partaking of all the sufferings of her Son in her blessed soul and in her body.

At noon the executioners, intending to crucify Jesus naked, despoiled Him of the seamless tunic and of His garments. As the tunic was large and without opening in front, they pulled it over the head of Jesus without taking off the crown of thorns; but on account of the rudeness with which they proceeded, they inhumanly tore off the crown with the tunic. Thus they opened again all the wounds of His head, and in some of them remained the thorns, which, in spite of their being so hard and sharp, were wrenched off by the violence with which the executioners despoiled Him of his tunic and, with it, of the crown. With heartless cruelty they again forced it down upon his sacred head, opening up wounds upon wounds. By tearing off the tunic the wounds of his whole body were renewed since the tunic had dried into the open places and its removal was adding new pains to His wounds. Four times during the Passion did they despoil Jesus of His garments and again vest Him. The first time in order to scourge Him at the pillar; the second time in order to clothe Him in the mock purple; the third, when they took this off in order to clothe Him in His tunic; the fourth, when they finally took away His clothes. This was the most painful, because His wounds were numerous, His body was very weak and there was no shelter against the sharp wind on Mount Calvary; for also this element was permitted to increase the sufferings of His death-struggle by sending its cold blasts across the mount.

To all these sufferings was added the confusion of being bereft of his garments in the presence of his most blessed Mother, of her pious companions, and in full sight of the multitudes gathered around.

In order to find the places for the auger-holes on the Cross, the executioners commanded Jesus to stretch Himself out upon it. He obeyed without hesitation. But they marked the places for the holes, not according to the size of his body, but farther apart having in mind a new torture for their Victim; that His limbs should be wrenched from their sockets in being nailed to the Cross.

When He rose from the Cross, and they set about boring the holes, the great Lady approached and took hold of one of his hands, adoring Him and kissing it with greatest reverence. The executioners allowed this because they thought that the sight of his Mother would cause so much the greater affliction to the Lord; for they wished to spare Him no sorrow they could cause Him. But they were ignorant of the hidden mysteries; for the Lord during his Passion had no greater source of consolation and interior joy than to see in the soul of his most Blessed Mother, the beautiful likeness of Himself and the full fruits of his Passion and Death. This joy, to a certain extent, comforted Christ our Lord also in that hour.

Having bored the three holes into the Cross, the executioners again commanded Christ the Lord to stretch Himself out upon it in order to be nailed to it. Jesus obeyed and placed Himself with outstretched arms upon the wood.
One of the executioners took the hand of Jesus and placed it upon the auger-hole, while another hammered a large and rough nail through the palm. The veins and sinews were torn, and the bones of the hand were forced apart. When they stretched out the other hand, they found that it did not reach up to the auger-hole; for the sinews of the other arm had been shortened and the executioners had maliciously set the holes too far apart. In order to overcome the difficulty, they took the chain, with which the Savior had been bound in the garden, and looping one end through a ring around His wrist, they pulled His hand over the hole and fastened it with another nail.

Thereupon they seized His feet, and placing them one above the other, they tied the same chain around both and stretched them with barbarous ferocity down to the third hole. Then they drove through both feet a large nail into the Cross. Thus His sacred body was nailed motionless to the Cross and was so stretched that the bones of His body, dislocated and forced from their natural position, could all be counted. The bones of His breast, of His shoulders and arms, and of His whole body were torn from their sinews.

After the Savior was nailed to the Cross, the executioners judged it necessary to bend the points of the nails which projected through the back of the wood, in order that they might not be loosened and drawn out by the weight of the body. For this purpose, they raised up the Cross in order to turn, it over, so that the body of Jesus would rest face downward upon the ground with the weight of the Cross upon Him. This new cruelty appalled all the bystanders and a shout of pity arose in the crowd. But the sorrowful and compassionate Blessed Mother intervened by her prayers, and asked the Eternal Father not to permit this boundless, outrage to happen in the way the executioners had intended. She commanded her holy angels to come to the assistance of their Creator. When, therefore, the executioners raised up the Cross to let it fall, with the crucified Lord Jesus face downward upon the ground, the holy angels supported Him and the Cross above the stony ground, so that His face did not come in contact with the rocks and pebbles. Altogether ignorant of the miracle, the executioners bent over the points of the nails; for Jesus' body was so near to the ground and the Cross was so firmly held by the angels, that the Jews thought it rested upon the hard rock.

Then they dragged the lower end of the Cross with the crucified Jesus near to the hole, wherein it was to be planted. Some of them getting under the upper part of the Cross with their shoulders, others pushing upward with their axes and lances, they raised the Savior on His Cross and fastened its foot in the hole they had drilled into the ground. Thus our true life and salvation now hung in the air upon the sacred wood in full view of the innumerable multitudes of different nations and countries.

The executioners placed the sharp points of their lances and axes to His body and fearfully lacerating Him under the armpits in helping to push the Cross into position. At this spectacle new cries of protest arose with still more vehemence and confusion from the multitude of people. The Jews blasphemed, the kind-hearted lamented, the strangers were astounded, some of them called the attention of the bystanders to the proceedings, others turned away their heads in horror and pity, others took to themselves a warning from this spectacle of suffering, and still others proclaimed Him a just Man.

Then they crucified the two thieves and planted their crosses to the right and the left of Jesus the Savior; for thereby they wished to indicate that He deserved the most conspicuous place as being the greatest malefactor. The pharisees and priests threw stones and dirt at the Cross of the Lord Jesus and His Body saying: "Ah Thou, who destroys the temple and in three days rebuild it, save now Thyself; others He has made whole, Himself He cannot save; if this be the Son of God let Him descend from the Cross, and we will believe in Him" (Matt. 27, 42). The two thieves in the beginning also mocked the Lord Jesus and said: "If Thou art the Son of God, save Thyself and us."

By the commands of the Blessed Virgin Mary, the Power of God had provided for all that was to happen at the death of His Onlybegotten Son. The Lord Jesus enlightened and moved the hearts of many of the bystanders at the time of these happenings on earth, and even before that time, in order that they might confess Jesus crucified as holy, just and as the true Son of God. Among them were not only those who previously had heard and believed His doctrine, but also a great number of such as had never seen Him or witnessed His miracles. For the same reason Pilate was also inspired not to change the title of the Cross which they had placed over the head of the Savior in Hebrew, Greek and Latin. For when the Jews protested and asked Him not to write: "Jesus of Nazareth, King of the Jews" but: "This one says, He is King of the Jews", Pilate answered: "What is written, is written, and I do not wish it to be changed."

All the inanimate creatures, by divine will, obeyed the command of the Blessed Virgin Mary. From the noon hour until three o clock in the afternoon, which was called the ninth hour, when the Lord expired, great disturbances and changes occurred as mentioned in the Gospels. The sun hid its light, the planets showed great alterations, the earth quaked, many mountains were leveled; the rocks shook one against the other, the graves opened and sent forth some of the dead alive. The changes in the elements and in the whole universe were so notable and extraordinary that they were evident on the whole earth. All the Jews of Jerusalem were dismayed and astonished; although their treachery and malice made them unworthy of the truth and hindered them from accepting what all the insensible creatures displayed to them.

The soldiers who had crucified Jesus, according to a custom permitting the executioners to take possession of the property of those whom they executed, now proceeded to divide the garments of Jesus. The cloak or outside mantle, which by divine disposition they had brought to Mount Calvary and which was the one Jesus had laid aside at the washing of the feet, they divided among themselves, cutting it into four parts (John 19, 23). But the seamless tunic, by a mysterious decree of Providence, they did not divide, but they drew lots and assigned it entirely to the one who drew the lot for it; thus fulfilling the prophecy in the twenty-first Psalm.

Jesus spoke those words of highest charity and perfection: "Father, forgive them, for they know not what they do!" (Luke 23, 34.) One of the two thieves, called Dismas became aware of some of the mysteries. Being assisted at the same time by the prayers and intercession of the Blessed Virgin Mary, he was interiorly enlightened concerning his Rescuer and Master by the first word on the Cross. Moved by true sorrow and contrition for his sins, Dismas turned to his companion and said: "Do you not fear God, seeing that you are under the same condemnation? We justly deserve our punishment for our deeds, but this Man has done no evil." And thereupon speaking to Jesus, he said: "Lord, remember me when You shall come into Thy kingdom!" (Luke 23, 40.) And Jesus said to Dismas: "Amen, I say to thee, this day you shall be with Me in Paradise."

Having justified the good thief, Jesus turned to His afflicted Mother, who with St. John was standing at the foot of the Cross. Speaking to both, he first addressed His Mother, saying: "Woman, behold thy son!" and then to St. John: "Behold thy Mother!" (John 19, 26.) St. John on his part received Her as his own Mother from that hour on. The Blessed Virgin Mary accepted St. John as her son.

Already the ninth hour of the day was approaching, although the darkness and confusion of nature made it appear to be rather a chaotic night. Jesus spoke the fourth word from the Cross in a loud and strong voice, so that all the bystanders could hear it: "My God, my God, why hast thou forsaken Me?" (Matt. 27, 46.) Although the Lord had uttered these words in his own Hebrew language, they were not understood by anyone except the Blessed Virgin Mary.

Jesus intimated quite a different meaning by these words of complaint, one which originated from His immense love for men; namely, from His love for those that He could not save which during His last hour caused in Him the same horrific anguish as it did during His prayer in the Garden of Gethsemane where He sweat blood. He grieved that His superabundant act of Redemption, offered for the whole human race, would not save all of mankind. As a consequence of the Decree of His Father's Eternal Will, He lovingly and sorrowfully complained of it in the words: "My God, my God, why hast Thou forsaken Me?" that is, in so far as the Eternal Father deprived Him of the salvation of the unrepentant sinners.

In confirmation of this sorrow the Lord Jesus added: "I thirst!" The sufferings of the Lord and his anguish could easily cause a natural thirst. But for Him this was not a time to complain of this thirst or to quench it; and therefore Jesus would not have spoken of it so near to His expiration, unless in order to give expression to a most exalted mystery.

He was thirsting to see the captive children of Adam make use of the liberty, which He merited for them and offered to them, and which so many were abusing. He was athirst with the anxious desire that all should correspond with Him in the faith and love due Him, that they profit by His merits and sufferings, accept His friendship and grace now acquired for them, and that they should not lose the eternal happiness which He was to leave as an inheritance to those that wished to merit and accept it. This was the thirst of Jesus our Savior; and the Blessed Virgin Mary alone understood it perfectly and began, with ardent affection and charity, to invite and interiorly to call upon all the poor, the afflicted, the humble, the despised and downtrodden to approach Jesus their Savior and thus quench, at least in part, His thirst which they could not quench entirely. But the treacherous Jews and executioners, fastened a sponge soaked in gall and vinegar to a reed and mockingly raised it to his mouth, in order that He might drink of it. Thus was fulfilled the prophecy of David: "In my thirst they gave me vinegar to drink" (John 16, 28; Ps. 68, 22). Our most patient Savior tasted of it, partaking of this drink in mysterious submission to the condemnation of the unrepentant sinners.

In connection with this same mystery the Savior then pronounced the sixth word: "Consummatum est." "It is consummated." (John 19, 29). Now is consummated this work of my coming from heaven and I have obeyed the command of My Eternal Father, who sent Me to suffer and die for the salvation of mankind. Now are fulfilled the holy Scriptures, the prophecies and figures of the old Testament, and the course of My earthly and mortal life assumed in the womb of My Mother. Now are established on earth my example, my doctrines, my Sacraments and my remedies for the sickness of sin. Now is appeased the justice of My Eternal Father in regard to the debt of the children of Adam. Now is my holy Church enriched with the remedies for the sins committed by men ; the whole work of my coming into the world is perfected in so far as concerns Me, its Restorer; the secure foundation of the triumphant Church is now laid in the Church militant, so that nothing can overthrow or change it. These are the mysteries contained in the few words: "Consummatum est."

Having finished and established the work of Redemption in all its perfection, it was becoming that the Incarnate Word, just as He came forth from the Father to enter mortal life should enter into immortal life of the Father through death. Then came Jesus' simple and humble recommendation to His Father saying: "Father, into thy hands I commend my spirit." The Lord spoke these words in a loud and strong voice, so that the bystanders heard them. In pronouncing them He raised his eyes to heaven, as one speaking with the Eternal Father, and with the last breath gave up His spirit and hung His head. By the divine force of these words Lucifer with all his demons were hurled into the deepest caverns of hell, there they lay motionless.

The Blessed Virgin Mary was the Mother of the Savior and the Co-redempterist of His Passion. In order that She might participate in it to the end, just as She had felt in her own body the other torments of her Son, though remaining alive, she felt and suffered the pains and agony of His death. She did not die in reality; but this was because God miraculously preserved her life, when according to the natural course death should have followed. This miraculous aid was more wonderful than all the other favors She received during the Passion. For this last pain was more intense and penetrating; and all that the martyrs and the men sentenced to death have suffered from the beginning of the world cannot equal what the Blessed Virgin Mary suffered during the Passion.

The Evangelist St. John tells us that near the Cross stood the Blessed Virgin Mary, with Mary Cleophas and Mary Magdalen. ... ...

It was the evening before the Sabbath of the Jews, and in order to celebrate it with unburdened minds, they had asked Pilate for permission to break the legs of the three men sentenced, so that, their death being hastened, they might be taken from the crosses and not left on them for the following day. With this intent the company of soldiers, which Mary now saw, had come to Mount Calvary. As they saw the two thieves were still alive, they broke their legs and so hastened their end (John 19, 31).

138

But when they examined Jesus they found Him already dead, and therefore did not break His legs thus fulfilling the mysterious prophecy in Exodus (Ex. 12, 46), commanding that no bones be broken in the figurative lamb to be eaten for the Passover. But a soldier, by the name of Longinus, approaching the Cross of Christ, thrust his lance into the side of Jesus the Savior. Immediately water and blood flowed from the wound, as St. John, who saw it and who gives testimony of the truth, assures us (John 19, 34).

This wounding of the lance, which could not be felt by the sacred and dead body of the Lord, was felt by the most blessed Mother in his stead and in the same manner as if her chaste bosom had been pierced. But even this pain was exceeded by the affliction of her most holy soul, in witnessing the cruel laceration of the breast of her dead Son. At the same time, moved by compassion and love and in forgetfulness of her own sorrow, She said to Longinus: "The Almighty look upon thee with eyes of mercy for the pain thou has caused to my soul!"

Thus it happened; for Jesus moved by the prayer of His Blessed Mother, ordained that some of the blood and water from His side should drop upon the face of Longinus and restore to him his eyesight, which he had almost lost. At the same time sight was given to his soul, so that he recognized in the Crucified Jesus his Savior, whom he had so inhumanly mutilated. Through this enlightenment Longinus was converted; weeping over his sins and having washed them in the blood and water of the side of Jesus Christ, he openly acknowledged and confessed Him as the true God and Savior of the world. He proclaimed Him as such in the presence of the Jews, confounding them by his testimony.

The Blessed Virgin Mary saw another group of men coming toward Calvary with ladders and other apparatus seemingly for the purpose of taking the body of Jesus from the Cross. But as She did not know their intentions, She was tortured by new fears of the cruelty of the Jews, and turning to St. John, She said: "My Son, what may be the object of these people in coming with all these instruments?"

139

St. John answered: "Do not fear them that are coming, my Lady; for they are Joseph and Nikodemus with some of their servants, all of them friends and servants of thy divine Son and my Lord." Joseph was just in the eyes of the Most High.

Although Joseph had been a secret disciple of Jesus, yet at His death, he openly confessed his fidelity. Setting aside all fear of the envy of the Jews and caring nothing for the power of the Romans, he went boldly to Pilate and asked for the body of Jesus (Mark 15, 43), in order to take Him down from the Cross and give Him a honorable burial. Jesus openly maintained that He was innocent and the true Son of God, as witnessed by the miracles of His life and death.

Pilate dared not refuse the request of Joseph, but gave him full permission to dispose of the dead body of Jesus as he thought fit. With this permission Joseph left the house of Pilate and called upon Nikodemus. He too was a just man, learned in divine and human letters and in the holy Scriptures, as is evident in what St. John related of him when he visited Christ at Night in order to hear the doctrine of Jesus Christ (John 3, 2). Joseph provided the winding sheets and burial cloths for the body of Jesus, while Nikodemus bought about one hundred pounds of the spices, which the Jews were accustomed to use in the burial of distinguished men (Matt.. 27, 59). Provided with these and with other necessities took their way to Calvary. They were accompanied by their servants and some other pious and devout persons, in whom likewise the blood shed for all by the crucified God had produced its salutary effects.
They approached most Holy Mary, who, in the company of St. John and the holy women, stood in inconceivable sorrow at the foot of the Cross. Instead of a salute, their sorrow at the sight of so painful a spectacle as that of the divine Crucified, was roused to such vehemence and bitterness, that Joseph and Nikodemus remained for a time prostrate at the feet of the Queen and all of them at the foot of the Cross without speaking a word. All of them wept and sighed most bitterly until the invincible Queen raised them from the ground and animated and consoled them; whereupon they saluted Her in humble compassion.

The most observant Mother thanked them kindly, especially for the service they were about to render to their God and Savior, and promised them the reward in the name of Him whose body they were to lay in the tomb. Joseph of Arimathea answered: "Even now, our Lady, do we feel in the secret of our hearts the sweet delight of the divine Spirit, who has moved us to such love, that we never could merit it or succeed in explaining it." Then they divested themselves of their mantles and with their own hands Joseph and Nikodemus placed the ladders to the holy Cross. On these they ascended in order to detach the sacred body, while the glorious Mother stood closely by leaning on the arms of saint John and Mary Magdalen. It seemed to Joseph, that the sorrow of the heavenly Lady would be renewed, when the sacred body should be lowered and She should touch it, and therefore He advised the Apostle to take Her aside in order to draw away her attention. But St. John, who knew better the invincible heart of the Queen, answered that from the beginning She had stood by to witness the torments of the Lord and that She would not leave him whom She venerated as her God and loved as the Son of her Womb.

Nevertheless, they continued to urge the expediency of her retiring for a short time, until they should lower their Master from the Cross. But the great Lady responded: "My dearest masters, since I was present, when my sweetest Son was nailed to the Cross, fear not to allow me to be present at His taking down; for this act of piety, though it shall affect my heart with new sorrow, will, in its very performance, afford a great relief." Thereupon they began to arrange for the taking down of the body. First they detached the crown from the head, laying bare the lacerations and deep wounds it had caused. They handed it down with great reverence and amid abundant tears, placing it in the hands of the sweetest Mother. She received it prostrate on her knees, in deepest adoration bathed it with her tears, permitting the sharp thorns to wound her virginal countenance in pressing it to her face. She asked the Eternal Father to inspire due veneration toward the sacred thorns in those Christians, who should obtain possession of them in future times.

In imitation of the Mother, St. John with the pious women and the other faithful there present, also adored it; and this they also did with the nails, handing them first to most holy Mary for veneration and afterward showing their own reverence. Then the great Lady placed Herself on her knees and held the unfolded cloth in her outstretched arms ready to receive the dead body of her Son. In order to assist Joseph and Nikodemus, saint John supported the head, and Mary Magdalen the feet of Christ and thus they tearfully and reverently placed Him into the arms of his sweetest Mother. This was to Her an event of mixed sorrow and consolation; for in seeing Him thus wounded and all His beauty disfigured beyond all children of men (Ps. 44, 3), the sorrows of her most chaste heart were again renewed; and in holding Him in her arms and at her breast, her incomparable sorrow was rejoiced and her love satiated by the possession of her Treasure. She looked upon Him with supreme worship and reverence, shedding tears of blood. In union with Her, as He rested in her arms, all the multitude of her attendant angels worshipped Him, although unseen by all others except Mary. Then St. John first, and after him all those present in their turn, adored the sacred Body. The most prudent Mother, seated on the ground, in the meanwhile held Him in her arms in order that they might satisfy their devotion.

Some time passed during which the sorrowful Mother held at her breast the dead Jesus, and as evening was far advancing, saint John and Joseph besought Her to allow the burial of her Son and God to proceed. The most prudent Mother yielded; and they now embalmed the sacred body, using all the hundred pounds of the spices and the aromatic ointments brought by Nikodemus. Thus anointed, the deified body was placed on a bier, in order to be carried to the sepulchre.

A procession of heavenly spirits was formed and another of men, and the sacred body was borne along by St. John, Joseph, Nikodemus and the centurion Longinus who had confessed the Lord and now assisted at his burial. They were followed by the blessed Mother, by Mary Magdalen and the rest of the women disciples. Besides these a large number of the faithful assisted, for many had been moved by the divine light and had come to Calvary after the lance-thrust.

All of them, in silence and in tears, joined the procession. They proceeded toward a nearby garden, where Joseph had hewn into the rock a new grave, in which nobody had as yet been buried or deposited (John 19, 41). In this sepulchre they placed the sacred body of Jesus. Before they closed it up with the heavy stone, the devout and prudent Mother adored Christ anew, causing the admiration of men and angels. They imitated Her, all of them adoring the crucified Savior now resting in His grave; thereupon they closed the sepulchre with a very heavy stone.

19. Resurrection

The divine soul of Christ our Redeemer remained in limbo from half past three of Friday afternoon, until after three of the Sunday morning following. During this hour He returned to the Sepulchre as the victorious Saviour of the angels and of the saints, whom He had delivered from those nether prisons as spoils of His victory and as an earnest of His glorious triumph over the chastised and prostrate rebels of hell. In the sepulchre were many angels as its guard, venerating the sacred body united to the Divinity. Obeying the command of the Blessed Virgin Mary, some of the angels had gathered the relics of the sacred blood shed by her divine Son, the particles of flesh scattered about, the hair torn from his divine face and head, and all else that belonged to the perfection and integrity of His most sacred humanity. The angels took charge of these relics, each one filled with joy at being privileged to hold the particles, which he was able to secure. Before any change was made, the body of the Redeemer was shown to the holy Fathers, in the same wounded, lacerated and disfigured state in which it was left by the cruelty of the Jews. Beholding Him thus disfigured in death, the Patriarchs and Prophets and other saints adored Him and again confessed Him as the Incarnate Word, who had truly taken upon Himself our infirmities and sorrows (Is. 53, 4) and paid abundantly our debts, satisfying in His innocence for what we ourselves owed to the justice of the Eternal Father.

Then, in the presence of all those saints, through the ministry of the angels, were united to the sacred body all the relics, which they had gathered, restoring it to its natural perfection and integrity. In the same moment the most holy soul reunited with the body, giving it immortal life and glory. Instead of the winding-sheets and the ointments, in which it had been buried, it was clothed with the four gifts of glory, namely: with clearness, impassibility, agility and subtility (John 19, 40).

The gifts of the Resurrection were transportability, impassibility, and subtility. Jesus could transport Himself body and soul instantaneously to anywhere.

144

Through impassibility His body became invincible to all created power, since no power can ever move or change Him. By subtility the gross and earthly matter was so purified, that it could now penetrate other matter like a pure spirit.

Accordingly, He penetrated through the rocks of the sepulchre without removing or displacing them, just as He had issued forth from the womb of His Blessed Mother. Agility so freed Him from the weight and slowness of matter, that it exceeded the agility of the immaterial angels, while He himself could move about more quickly than they, as shown in His apparitions to the Apostles and on other occasions. The sacred wounds, which had disfigured His body, now shone forth from his hands and feet and side so refulgent and brilliant, that they added a most entrancing beauty and charm. In all this glory and heavenly adornment Jesus the Savior now arose from the grave; and in the presence of the saints and Patriarchs He promised universal resurrection in their own flesh and body to all men, and that they moreover, as an effect of His own Resurrection, should be glorified like Him. As a pledge of the universal resurrection, the Lord commanded the souls of many saints there present to reunite with their bodies and rise up to immortal life.

Immediately this divine command was executed, and their bodies arose, as is mentioned by St. Matthew, in anticipation of this mystery (Matthew 27, 52). Among them was St. Anne, St. Joseph and St. Joachim, and others of the ancient Fathers and Patriarchs, who had distinguished themselves in the faith and hope of the Incarnation, and had desired and prayed to God for it. As a reward for their devotion, the resurrection and glory of their bodies was now anticipated. At Jesus' command the dry and scattered bones of the ancient dead were joined together, and the flesh, which had long ago turned to dust, was united to the bones, renewed their former life, and adorned by the gifts of glory communicated to it by the life-restoring soul.

In one instant all these saints gathered around Jesus their Savior, more refulgent and brilliant than the sun, pure, transparent, beautiful and agile, fit to follow Him everywhere and by their own good fortune they now confirmed the prophecy of Job, that, in our own flesh and with our own eyes, and not with those of others, we shall see our Redeemer for our consolation (Job 19, 26). In all these mysteries the Blessed Virgin Mary was aware and participated in them from her retreat in the Cenacle (e.g. 'the upper room').

After Jesus our Savior, arisen and glorified, had visited and filled with glory his most blessed Mother, He resolved, as the loving Father and Pastor, to gather the sheep of his flock, which the scandal of his sufferings had disturbed and scattered. The holy Patriarchs and all whom He had rescued from limbo continually remained in his company, although they did not manifest themselves and remained invisible during his apparitions; only our great Queen was privileged to see them, know them and speak to them all during the forty days between the Resurrection and the Ascension of her divine Son. Whenever the Lord did not appear to others, He remained with his beloved Mother in the Cenacle; nor did She ever leave this place during all the forty days. There She enjoyed the presence of Jesus the Redeemer of the world and of the choir of Prophets and Saints, by whom Jesus and Mary were attended. For the purpose of making His Resurrection known to His Apostles, Jesus began by appearing to the women, not on account of their weakness, but because they were stronger in their belief and in their hope of the Resurrection; for this is the reason why they merited the privilege of being the first to see Him arisen.

Mary Magdalen and Mary Cleophas with other holy women, went forth on the evening of the sabbath from the Cenacle to the city and bought additional ointments and spices in order to return, early the following morning, to the sepulchre, and show their veneration by visiting and anointing the holy body once more. On the Sunday, entirely ignorant of the tomb's having been sealed and placed under guard by order of Pilate (Matt. 27, 65), they arose before dawn in order to execute their pious design.

146

On their way they thought only of the difficulty of removing the large stone, which they now remembered had been rolled before the opening of the sepulchre; but their love made light of this hindrance, though they did not know how to remove it.

When they came forth from the house of the Cenacle, it was yet dark, but before they arrived at the sepulchre the sun had already dawned and risen; for on that day the three hours of darkness which had intervened at the Death of the Savior, were compensated by an earlier sunrise. This miracle will harmonize the statements of St. Mark and of St. John, of whom the one says, that the Marys came after sunrise, and the other that it was yet dark (Mark 16, 2; John 20, 1); for both speak truly: That they went forth very early and before dawn, and that the sun, by its more sudden and accelerated flight, had already risen at their arrival at the grave, though they tarried not on the short way. The sepulchre was in an arched vault, as in a cave, the entrance to which was covered by a large stone slab. Within, somewhat to one side and raised from the ground, was the hollow slab wherein the body of the Savior rested.

A little before the Marys thought and spoke of the difficulty of removing the stone, a violent and wonderful quaking or trembling of the earth took place; at the same time an angel of the Lord opened the sepulchre and cast aside the stone that covered and obstructed the entrance (Matt. 28, 2). At this noise of the earthquake the guards of the sepulchre fell prostrate to the earth, struck motionless with fear and consternation, although they did not see the Lord. For the body of the Lord was no more in the grave; He had already arisen and came forth from the tomb before the angel cast aside the stone. The Marys, though in some fear, took heart and were encouraged by God to approach and enter the vault. Near the entrance they saw the angel who had thrown aside the stone, seated upon it, refulgent in countenance and in snow-white garments (Mark 16, 5). He spoke to them saying: "Do not be afraid; you seek Jesus of Nazareth, who was crucified: He is risen, He is not here; behold the place where they laid Him."

147

The holy women entered, and seeing the sepulchre vacant they were filled with grief; for as yet they were more deeply affected at seeing the Lord absent, than by the words of the angel. Then they saw two other angels seated at each end of the slab, who said to them: "Why seek you the Living with the dead? Remember how He spoke unto you, when he was yet in Galilee (Luke 26, 4-5), that He was to rise on the third day. But go, tell his disciples and Peter, that He goes before you into Galilee, there shall you see Him" (Mark 16, 7).
Being reminded by the angels the Marys remembered what Jesus had said. Assured of His Resurrection they hurried away from the sepulchre and gave an account to the eleven Apostles and other disciples of the Lord Jesus. But many of these were so shaken and so forgetful of the words of Jesus, that they thought this story of the holy women a mere hallucination (Luke 24, 11). While the holy women, full of trembling and joy, related to the Apostles what they had seen, the centurions at the grave awoke from their stupor and regained the use of their senses. As they saw the sepulchre open and emptied of the sacred body, they fled to give notice of the event to the pharisees and priests (Matt. 11, 14). These were cast into great consternation and called a meeting in order to determine what they could do in order to palliate the miracle, which was so patent that it could not remain hidden. They concluded to offer to the soldiers much money to induce them to say that during their sleep the disciples of Jesus had come and stolen the body from the grave.

The priests, having assured the guards of immunity and protection, spread this lie among the Jews. Many were so foolish as to believe it; and there are some in our own day, who are obstinate and blind enough to give it credit and who prefer to accept the testimony of witnesses, who acknowledged that they were asleep during the time of which they testify.

Although the disciples and Apostles considered the tale of the Marys preposterous, St. Peter and St. John, desirous of convincing themselves with their own eyes, quickly departed to the sepulchre, closely followed by the holy women (John 20, 3). St. John arrived first, and without entering saw the buriel wrappings neatly folded and laid to one side.

He waited for the arrival of St. Peter, who, passing the other Apostle, entered first. Both of them saw that the sacred body was not in the tomb. St. John then was assured of what he had begun to believe, when he had seen the great change in appearance of the Blessed Virgin Mary, and he then professed his belief. The two Apostles returned to give an account of the wonder they had seen in the sepulchre. The Marys remained in a place apart from the sepulchre and wonderingly commented on the events. Mary Magdalen, in great excitement and tears, re-entered the sepulchre to reconnoiter. Although the Apostles had not seen the angels, she saw them and they asked her: "Woman, why dost thou weep?" (John 20, 5). She answered: "Because they have taken away my Lord; and I know not where they have laid Him." With this answer she left the garden where the sepulchre was, and met the Lord. She did not know Him, but thought it was the gardener. And the Lord also asked her: "Woman, why weep thou? Whom dost thou seek?" (John 15). Magdalen, ignorant of his being the Lord, answered Him as if He were the gardener and, without further reflection, said: "Sir, if thou hast taken Him hence, tell me where thou hast laid Him, and I will take Him away." Then the loving Master said: "Mary" and in pronouncing her name He permitted Himself to be recognized by the tone of his voice. As soon as Magdalen recognized Jesus she was aflame with joyous love and answered saying: "Rabboni, my Master!" Throwing herself at His feet, she was about to touch and kiss them, as being used to that favor. But the Lord prevented her and said: "Do not touch Me, for I am not yet ascended to My Father whence I came; but return and tell My brethren, the Apostles, that I am going to My Father and theirs."

Then Magdalen left, filled with consolation and jubilee. Shortly she met the other Marys. Scarcely had they heard what had happened to her and how she had seen Jesus arisen from the grave, and while they were yet standing together conferring with each other in wonder and tears of joy, He appeared to them and said: "God save you." They all recognized Him and, as St. Matthew tells us, they worshipped his sacred feet.

The Lord again commanded them to go to the Apostles and tell them, that they had seen Him and that they should go to Galilee, where they should see Him arisen (Matt. 22, 9). Jesus then disappeared and the holy women hastened to the Cenacle to tell the Apostles all that had happened to them; but the Apostles continued to hesitate in their belief (Luke 24, 11). Then the women sought the Queen of Heaven in order to tell Her of the events. Although Mary knew all that had happened by intellectual vision, She listened to them with admirable tenderness and prudence. While listening to the Marys, she took occasion to confirm their faith in the mysteries and high sacraments of the Incarnation and in the passages of Holy Scriptures pertaining thereto. But the heavenly Queen did not tell them what had happened, although She was the Teacher of these faithful and devout disciples, just as the Lord was the Teacher of the Apostles in holy faith.

After Jesus had appeared to the women. He appeared to St. Peter in private as the head of the Church and before He appeared to all of the Apostles together or to any one of them. This happened on that same day, after the holy women had informed him of His apparition to them. Soon after also happened the apparition of the Lord to the two disciples going that afternoon to Emmaus, which is described in detail in the Gospels. These two disciples quickly returned to the Cenacle in Jerusalem to proclaim to the Apostles that they have seen the Lord Jesus. Shortly after, when Thomas had left and the doors had been locked, the Lord entered and appeared to the others. In their midst He saluted them, saying: "Peace be with you. It is I; do not fear."

At this sudden apparition, the Apostles feared lest what they saw was a ghost, and the Lord added: "Why are you troubled, and why do thoughts arise in your hearts? See my hands and feet, that it is I myself; handle and see: for a spirit hath no flesh and bones, as you see Me have." The Apostles were so excited and confused, that though they saw Him and touched the wounded hands of the Savior, they could not realize, that it was He to whom they spoke and whom they touched.
The loving Master in order to assure them still more, said to them: "Give Me to eat, if you have aught." Joyfully they offered Him some fried fish and a comb of honey.

He ate part of these, and divided the rest among them, saying: "Do you not know, that all that has happened with Me is the same that has been written by Moses and the Prophets, in the Psalms and holy Scriptures, and that all must necessarily be fulfilled in Me as it was prophesied?" And at these words He opened their minds, and they knew Him, and understood the sayings of the Scriptures concerning his Passion, Death and Resurrection on the third day. Having thus instructed them, He said again: "Peace be with you. As the Father has sent me, so I send you, in order that you may teach the world the knowledge of the truth, of God and of eternal life, preaching repentance for sins and forgiveness of them in my name." Breathing upon them, He added and said: "Receive ye the Holy Spirit, in order that the sins which you forgive may be forgiven, and those which you do not forgive, may not be forgiven. Preach ye to all nations, beginning in Jerusalem." Then the Savior, having thus consoled and confirmed them in faith, and having given them and all priests the power to forgive sins, disappeared from their midst.All this took place in the absence of Thomas, but soon after he returned to the assembly, and the Apostles told him what had happened during His absence. Yet, though he found them so changed in joyful exultation, he remained incredulous and obstinate, maintaining, that he would not believe what all of them affirmed, unless he himself should see with his own eyes and touch with his own hands and fingers the wounds of the Savior's side and those of the nails (John 20, 25). In this obstinacy the incredulous Thomas persevered for eight days, when the Savior again returned through locked doors and appeared in the midst of the Apostles including Thomas. He saluted them as usual, saying: "Peace be with you," and then calling Thomas, He sweetly reprimanded him. "Come, Thomas, and with your hands touch the openings of my hands and of my side, and be not so incredulous, but convinced and believing." Thomas touched the divine wounds and was enlightened to believe and acknowledge his ignorance. Prostrating himself to the ground he said: "My Lord and my God!" to which the Lord replied: "Because thou hast seen Me, thou hast believed; but blessed are those who do not see Me and believe Me." The Lord then disappeared, leaving the Apostles and Thomas filled with light and joy.

151

20. Ascension [the last secret]

[Editor's note: The Gospels provide details of Jesus' Ascension to Heaven, thus for brevity the editor chooses to provide herein details of what occurred involving the Blessed Virgin Mary during the Ascension.]

Jesus with one hundred twenty of His disciples left the Cenacle, and, with his most blessed Mother at his side, He conducted them all through the streets of Jerusalem. The Apostles and all the rest in their order, proceeded in the direction of Bethany, which was about one mile to the Mount of Olives. The company of angels and saints from limbo and purgatory followed Jesus with new songs of praise, although only the Blessed Virgin Mary was privileged to see them. The Resurrection of Jesus of Nazareth had spread throughout Jerusalem and Israel. Although the deceitful and malicious pharisees and priests had spread about the false testimony of Jesus' body being stolen by His disciples, yet many would not accept their testimony, nor give it any credit. It was divinely provided, that none of the inhabitants of the city, and none of the unbelievers or doubters, should pay any attention to this holy procession, or hinder it on its way from the Cenacle. All, except the one hundred and twenty disciples, who were chosen by the Lord to witness His Ascension into heaven, were justly punished by being prevented from noticing this wonderful mystery, and the Chieftain and Head of this procession remained invisible to them.

The Lord having secured His disciples this privacy, together they all ascended the Mount of Olives to its highest point. There they formed three choirs, one of the angels, another of the saints, and a third of the Apostles and disciples which again divided into two bands, while Jesus the Savior presided. The Most High enabled the Blessed Mother miraculously to be in two places at once; remaining with the disciples for their comfort during their stay in the Cenacle and at the same time ascending with the Redeemer of the world to His heavenly throne, where She remained for three days. In heaven she enjoyed the use of all her powers and faculties, whereas on earth she was restricted in the use of them during that same time in the Cenacle.

Then the voice of the Eternal Father was heard saying: "My Daughter, ascend higher!" Her divine Son also called Her, saying: "My Mother, rise up and take possession of the place, which I owe Thee for having followed and imitated Me." The Holy Spirit said: "My Spouse and Beloved, come to my eternal embraces!" Immediately was proclaimed to all the blessed the decree of the most holy Trinity, by which the Blessed Mother, for having furnished her own life-blood toward the Incarnation and for having nourished, served, imitated and followed Him with all the perfection possible to a creature, was exalted and placed at the right hand of her Son for all eternity as an equal Sovereign.

When the disciples saw Jesus their beloved Master and Redeemer disappearing through the aerial regions and had almost lost sight of Him, a most resplendent cloud interposed itself between Him and those He had left upon earth (Acts 1, 9), intercepting Him altogether from their view. In it the Person of the Eternal Father descended from heaven to the regions of the air in order to meet the Son and the Mother, who had furnished the new mode of existence in which He now returned. Coming to Them the Eternal Father received Them in His embrace of infinite love, to the joy of the angels, who had accompanied the Father in innumerable choirs from His heavenly seat. In a short space of time, penetrating the elements and the celestial orbs, that whole divine procession arrived at the supreme regions of the empyrean heaven. At their entrance were the angels, who had ascended from the earth with their Sovereigns Jesus and Mary, and those who had joined them in the aerial regions.

Amid the jubilation of the angels and saints, the procession approached the empyrean heavens. Between the two choirs of angels and saints, Jesus and His Blessed Mother made their entry. All in their order gave supreme honor to Each respectively and to Both together, breaking forth in hymns of praise. Then the Eternal Father placed upon the throne of His Divinity at His right hand, the Incarnate Word, and in such glory and majesty, He filled with new admiration and reverential fear all the inhabitants of heaven. ...

On this occasion the humility and wisdom of our most prudent Queen reached their highest point; for, overwhelmed by such divine and admirable favors, She hovered at the footstool of the royal throne, annihilated in the consciousness of being a mere earthly creature. Prostrate She adored the Father and broke out in new canticles of praise for the glory communicated to his Son and for elevating in Him the deified humanity to such greatness and splendor. Again the angels and saints were filled with admiration and joy to see the most prudent humility of their Queen.

In fulfillment of this decree, the Eternal Father picked up the Blessed Virgin Mary and sat her on the throne of the Holy Trinity at the right hand of her Son and declared her a Sovereign of the universe; giving her equal power to the power of the Most High and the power to create or uncreate. At the same time She, with all the saints, was informed, that She was given possession of this throne not only for all the ages of eternity, but that it was left to her choice to remain there even now and without returning to the earth. For it was the conditional will of the divine Persons, that as far as they were concerned, She should now remain in that state. In order that She might make her own choice, She was shown anew the state of the Church upon earth, the orphaned condition of the faithful, whom She was left free to assist. Therefore, the Blessed Virgin Mary clearly saw before her eyes all the sacrifices included in this proposition, left the throne and, prostrating Herself at the feet of the Three Persons, said: "Eternal and almighty God, my Lord, to accept at once this reward, which thy generosity offers me, would be to secure my rest; but to return to the world and continue to labor in mortal life for the good of the children and Thy holy Church, would be to the glory and to the pleasure of thy Majesty and would benefit my sojourning and banished children on earth. I accept this labor ..."

The Most High renewed in Her all His gifts and confirmed and sealed them anew in the degree then befitting, in order to send Her back as a Mother and Teacher of the holy Church, confirming all the titles He had conferred upon Her as the Queen of all creation and a Sovereign of the universe and Mother of God.

After the disciples were told by the two angels, "Ye men of Galilee, do not look up to heaven in so great astonishment, for this Lord Jesus, who departed from you and has ascended into heaven, shall again return with the same glory and majesty in which you have just seen Him" (Acts 1, 11). They left the Mount of Olives and returned to the Cenacle with the Blessed Virgin Mary, although she was very silent and reserved as she was more in Heaven than on earth. For three days, the Blessed Virgin Mary remained in the Empyrean Heaven seated on the throne of the Blessed Trinity at the right hand of Jesus.

21. God's Wrath that was Inflicted by the Holy Spirit. (1st Pentecost Sunday)

In addition to the wonderful events described in the Bible in the Acts of the Apostles, that day, with the coming of the Holy Spirit in Jerusalem, was accompanied by tremendous thunder and lightning. The Holy Spirit unleashed the Wrath of the Most High on the enemies of the Lord Jesus. He disturbed, terrified and slaughtered the enemies of the Lord in that city, each one according to his own treachery.

This chastisement was particularly evident in those who had actively conspired in the death of the Lord Jesus, and who had identified themselves in their rabid fury against Him. All these fell to the ground on their faces and remained there for three hours, including all of the pharisees and especially those who judged the Lord. Those that had so cruelly scourged the Lord were suddenly choked in their own blood, which shot forth from their veins in punishment for shedding the sacred blood of Jesus. The arrogant servant that slapped and spit upon the sacred face of the Lord Jesus, not only suddenly died, but was hurdled into hell body and soul. Other Jews, that were not executed, were chastised with intense pains and abominable sicknesses. These torments were the consequences for shedding the precious blood of Jesus Christ, causing them to lay prostrate for three hours and even to this day continues to afflict their descendants with the most horrible maladies. This chastisement was immense in Jerusalem, although the priests and pharisees diligently tried to cover it up, just as they tried to conceal the Resurrection of Jesus. These events, were considered so unimportant, that neither the Apostles nor the Evangelists wrote about them, and in the chaos of the city all of the residents soon forgot these events.

The chastisement and terror extended also to the depths of hell, where Lucifer and the demons felt themselves seized with confusion and oppression for three days, just as the Jews lay facedown on the earth for three hours. During these three days Lucifer and his demons broke forth in fearful howlings, communicating new terror and confusion of torments to all of the damned.

22. Happenings of the Apostles

i. Apostles' Creed

After Jesus ascended to the right hand of the Father, He inspired St. Peter His vicar and the Apostles with the desire of setting up a symbol of the universal faith of the Church. Accordingly, they convened with the Blessed Virgin Mary concerning the measures to be taken for this purpose.

The Apostles with the Blessed Virgin Mary resolved to fast and pray for ten continuous days, in order to receive the inspiration of the Holy Spirit in this arduous matter. After the ten days, the twelve Apostles met in the presence of Mary, and St. Peter spoke to them as follows:
"My dear brethren, the divine mercy, in its infinite goodness and through the merits of our Savior and Master Jesus, has favored His Holy Church by multiplying its children, as we have seen and experienced in this short time. For this purpose, the Almighty has multiplied miracles and prodigies and daily renews them through our ministry, ... We must soon depart and preach throughout the world according to the command of the Lord Jesus before He ascended into heaven (Matt. 28, 19). We meet to ... define the truths and mysteries which we are to profess to all the nations, without difference of opinions, so all shall believe the same doctrines. ... that He will now assist us with His Divine Spirit to understand and define, in His name and by an unchangeable decree, the articles to be established in His holy Church ... to the end of the world."

All the Apostles consented to this proposal of St. Peter. Then he celebrated a Mass, in which he gave Communion to the Blessed Virgin Mary and the Apostles. After continuing their prayers to the Holy Spirit for some time, they heard the rumbling of thunder, as on the first coming down of the Holy Spirit upon the gathering of the faithful, at the same time the Cenacle was filled with light and splendor and all were enlightened by the Holy Spirit. Then the most blessed Mary asked each of the Apostles to define a mystery as the divine Spirit should inspire them.

In the following order each Apostle stated a doctrine of the Creed:

1. **St. Peter**: I believe in God, the Father almighty, Creator of heaven and earth.
2. **St. Andrew**: And in Jesus Christ, his only Son, our Lord.
3 & 4. **St. James the Greater**: Who was conceived through operation of the Holy Ghost, born of the Virgin Mary.
5. **St. John**: Suffered under Pontius Pilate, was crucified, died and was buried.
6 & 7. **St. Thomas**: Descended into hell, arose from the dead on the third day.
8. **St. James the Less**: Ascended into heaven, is seated at the right hand of God the Father almighty.
9. **St. Philip**: From thence He shall come to judge the living and the dead.
10. **St. Bartholomew**: I believe in the Holy Spirit.
11. **St. Matthew**: In the holy Catholic Church, the Communion of saints.
12. **St. Simon**: Forgiveness of sins.
13. **St. Thaddeus**: The resurrection of the body.
14. **St. Mathias**: Life everlasting. Amen.

This symbol, which we ordinarily call the Creed, the Apostles established after the martyrdom of St. Stephen and before the end of the first year after the death of the Savior.

As soon as the Apostles had finished pronouncing this Creed, the Holy Spirit approved of it by permitting a voice to be heard in their midst saying: "You have decided well." Then the Blessed Virgin Mary with all the Apostles gave thanks to the Most High; and she also thanked them for having merited the assistance of the Holy Spirit.

From this first recitation of the Apostles' Creed and for nearly three hundred years, the Holy Spirit would descend on whomever was reciting the Apostles' Creed as tongues of fire. This miracle happened at every recitation and ceased occurring sometime between 313 Edict of Milan and Nicaea Council of 325.

158

[Editor's note: God ceased His miracle of 'tongues of fire' most probably because the Church went from an impoverished, underground, outlawed, persecuted religion to a secular religion with great possessions.]

The written copies of the Creed of the Apostles were distributed in a very few days among the faithful to their incredible benefit and consolation; for in their fervor they received them with highest reverence and devotion. The Holy Ghost, who had ordained this Creed for the security of the Church, immediately began to confirm it by new miracles and prodigies, operating not only through the hands of the Apostles and disciples, but also through many of the believers. Many who received it with special veneration and love, were suddenly enveloped in divine splendor, filled with heavenly science and celestial manifestations of the Holy Spirit. By these miracles believers were moved to possess and reverence these documents. Other believers healed the sick, raised the dead and expelled demons from the possessed by merely placing the Credo upon them. Among other marvels it happened one day that a Jew, who was roused to anger at hearing a Christian devoutly reading the Creed and was about to tear it from his hands, fell dead.

From that time on, those that were baptized, being adults, were required to profess the faith according to the Apostles' Creed; and while they pronounced it, the Holy Spirit visibly appeared above them.

The gift of tongues likewise continued; for the Holy Spirit gave it not only on the day of Pentecost, but to many of the faithful afterwards who assisted in preaching or in giving instruction to the new believers; and whenever they spoke or preached to many different nationalities, they were understood by each nationality, though they spoke only in the Hebrew language. In like manner they were able to speak in other languages, when they happened upon a gathering of people all speaking the same foreign language.

Thus was renewed all that had happened at the first coming down of the Holy Spirit. Besides these miracles the Apostles performed many others, and whenever they laid their hands upon the believers, or confirmed them, the Holy Spirit descended upon them. So many miracles and prodigies were dispensed by the hands of the Almighty, that if they were all recorded, they would fill many volumes. Saint Luke in the Acts describes those in particular, which in justice should not be altogether left unnoticed in the Church of God. He adds in a general way, that they were very numerous, and therefore could not be included in his short history.

ii. St. Peter dispatches the Apostles to diverse locations

A full year had passed since the death of the Savior, and now the Apostles, by divine impulse, began to consider going forth to preach the faith throughout the world. In order to fulfill the will of God in the assignment of the kingdoms and provinces in which each one was to preach, upon the advice of the Blessed Mother, they resolved to fast and pray for ten days.

This practice of fasting and praying for ten days, they observed immediately after the Ascension in disposing themselves for the coming of the Holy Spirit.

At the end of their fast and prayer a wonderful light descended upon the Cenacle surrounding them all, and a voice was heard saying: "My vicar Peter shall point out the province, which falls to each one. I shall govern and direct him by my light and spirit." Peter hearing this voice, gave instructions to all the Apostles, as follows:

St. Peter: Jerusalem, provinces of Asia: Pontus, Galatia, Bythinia and Cappadocia; Antioch and finally Rome.

St. Andrew: Scythian provinces of Europe, Epirus and Thrace; City of Patras in Achaia.

St. James the greater: Judea, Samaria, Spain and return to Jerusalem.

St. John shall care and provide for the Blessed Virgin Mary as Jesus made known from the Cross. After she is taken to heaven, then Asia Minor governing the churches there established, and retire on the island of Patmos.

St.Thomas: India, Persia and the Parthians, Medes, Hircanians, Brahmans, Bactrians. He shall baptize the three Magi Kings and instruct them.

St. James: as Bishop of Jerusalem and assist John in the care of the Blessed Virgin Mary.

St. Philip: provinces Phrygia and Scythia of Asia, and in the city called Hieropolis in Phrygia.

St. Bartholomew: Lycaonia, part of Cappadocia in Asia; and to further India and afterwards to Armenia Minor.

St. Matthew: to Egypt and Ethiopia.

St. Simon: to Babylon, Persia and the kingdom of Ethiopia.

St. Thaddeus: Mesopotamia, and then join Simon to preach in Babylon and Persia.

St. Mathias: interior of Ethiopia, Arabia, and then Israel.

After Peter gave his instructions, a loud thunder was heard and the Cenacle was filled with refulgence in witness of the presence of the Holy Spirit. From the midst of this splendor was heard a soft voice saying: "Let each one accept his allotment." The Apostles prostrated themselves upon the ground and with one voice said: "Most High Lord, Thy word and the word of Thy vicar Peter we obey with a prompt and joyous heart, and our souls rejoice and are filled with the abundance of Thy wonderful works."

23. Latter years of the Blessed Virgin Mary

i. The Blessed Virgin Mary established the first building of a church "Our Lady of Pillar" in Saragossa Spain.

[Editor's note: Perhaps one of the greatest physical proofs provided by the Blessed Virgin Mary is the first century church of "Our Lady of Pillar" which she commanded St. James to build and contains the mystical pillar made by her angels that emits a heavenly fragrance even today and can be experienced by visitors.]

St. James the great was farther away than any of the others. He was the first one to leave Jerusalem, and, having preached some days in Judea, he departed for Spain. For this journey he embarked at Joppe, which is now called Jaffa, in the year thirty-five in the month of August, called Sextilis, one year and five months after the passion of the Lord, eight months after the martyrdom of St. Stephen and five months before the conversion of St. Paul,

Sailing from Jaffa, St. James touched at Sardinia and shortly afterwards arrived in Spain, disembarking at the port of Carthagena where he began his preaching. He tarried but a short time in Carthagena, and guided by the Spirit of the Lord, He took his way to Granada, where he was made aware that the harvest was bountiful and the occasion opportune for beginning his labors for his Master; and so it really turned out. St. James, the brother of St. John, needed the protection of the Blessed Virgin Mary, because he was of a generous and magnanimous heart, and of a most fervent spirit, being resistlessly drawn to offer himself for labors and dangers. Hence he was the first one to go forth preaching the faith and the first of all the Apostles to suffer martyrdom.

While the Blessed Mother continued in her prayers for St. James, four days before leaving for Ephesus, she saw her divine Son, descending in person to visit Her, seated upon a throne of ineffable majesty and accompanied by innumerable angels of all the heavenly choirs and hierarchies.

With all His court the Lord entered the oratory of His most Blessed Mother, ... Then the Lord spoke to her saying: "My most beloved Mother, ... The first one who is to imitate Me is my faithful servant James, and I wish that he suffer martyrdom in this city of Jerusalem. In order that he come here and for other purposes of my glory and thine, I desire thee to visit him in Spain, where he is preaching My name. I desire My Mother, that thou go to Saragossa where he now is, and command him to return to Jerusalem. But before he leaves that city, he is to build a church in thy name and title, where thou shalt be venerated and invoked for the welfare of that country, for my glory and pleasure, and that of the most Blessed Trinity."

The Blessed Virgin Mary accepted this commission from her divine Son with new joy. She answered: "My Lord and true God, let thy holy will be done ... Grant me, my Son, that in the church Thou commands to be built by Thy servant James, I may be permitted to promise the special protection of thy almighty arm, and that this sacred place shall be part of my inheritance for the use of all those that call with devotion upon thy holy name and ask me to intercede for them with thy clemency."

Jesus answered Her: "My Mother, in whom I am well pleased, I give thee my royal word, that I shall look with special clemency and fill with blessings all those who with devotion and humility call upon Me through thy intercession in that church. In thy hands have I deposited and consigned all My treasures; as My Mother, who holds My place and power, thou can signal that place by depositing therein thy riches and promising in it thy favors, for all will be fulfilled according to thy will and pleasure." Again the most Blessed Mary thanked her Son and God for this promise. Then, at the command of the Lord, a great number of the angels that accompanied Her formed a royal throne of a most resplendent cloud and placed Her thereon as the Queen of all Creation. Jesus the Savior gave them His blessing and ascended with the rest of the angels to heaven. The purest Mother, borne by the hands of the seraphim and accompanied by her thousand angels and the rest, departed body and soul for Saragossa in Spain.

163

Although this journey could have been made in the shortest moment of time, the Lord ordered the angels to move along singing hymns of praise and jubilee to their Queen in choirs of sweetest harmony.

Some of them sang the "Ave Maria," others "Salve Regina" others the "Regina coeli laetare," choir answering choir in such harmony and concord of sounds, as no human artist could ever attain. The Blessed Virgin Mary repeated many times: "Holy, holy, holy, Lord God Sabaoth (Is. 6, 3), have pity on the poor children of Eve. Thine is the glory, thine the power and majesty. Thou alone art holy, the Most High and the Lord of all the angelic armies and of all creation." The angels then would respond to these songs of their Queen proceeding in this manner till midnight when they arrived in Saragossa.
The most fortunate Apostle St. James was encamped with his disciples outside of the wall running along the banks of the river Ebro. In order to engage in prayer, he had separated some distance from his companions. Some of his disciples had fallen asleep and others were absorbed in prayer, all of them far from expecting the strange event. The procession of the angels spread out somewhat and sang still louder, so that not only St. James, but also his disciples could hear them from afar. Those that were asleep awoke and all of them were filled with wonder which caused them to remain speechless to shed tears of joy.

They saw in the sky a brilliant light, brighter than that of the sun, but it was not diffused beyond a certain space and seemed like a large luminous globe. Lost in admiration and joy they stood motionless until called by St. James. Through the miraculous effects, which they felt within them, the Lord wished to prepare them for what would be manifested to them concerning this great mystery. The holy angels placed the throne of their Queen and Lady within sight of the Apostle, who was still wrapped in most exalted prayer and heard much more plainly the celestial music and saw more of the light than his disciples. The angels bore with them a small column hewn of marble or jasper; and a small image of their Queen, made of some other material. This image was carried by the angels with great veneration.

164

During that night, the angels, exerting their skill in fashioning the things of nature, had prepared all this for the occasion. Seated on her throne in the cloud and surrounded by the angelic choirs the Blessed Virgin Mary manifested herself to St. James. In wonderful beauty and refulgence the great Lady far outshone all the angels. The blessed Apostle prostrated himself upon the earth and in deepest reverence venerated the Mother of his Creator and Redeemer. He was shown at the same time the image and the pillar or column in the hands of some of the angels. The loving Blessed Mother gave him her blessing in the name of her divine Son and said: "James, servant of the Most High, be thou blest by His right hand may He raise thee up and show thee the light of His divine countenance." All the angels answered: "Amen." The Blessed Mother continued: "My son James, this place the Most High and Omnipotent God of heaven has destined to be consecrated by thee upon earth for the erection of a church and house of prayer, where, under my patronage and name He wishes to be glorified and magnified, where the treasures of His right hand shall be distributed, and all His ancient mercies shall be opened up for the faithful through my intercession, if they ask for them in true faith and sincere piety. In the name of the Almighty I promise them great favors and blessings of sweetness, and my protection and assistance, for this is to be my house and temple, my inheritance and possession. A pledge of this truth and of my promise shall be this column with my image placed upon it. In the church which thou shalt build for me, it shall remain and be preserved, together with the holy faith, until the end of the world. Thou shalt immediately begin to build this church of God, and after thou hast completed it, thou shalt depart for Jerusalem; for my divine Son wishes thee to offer the sacrifice of thy life in the same place where He offered His for the salvation of the human race."

ii. Blessed Virgin Mary travels to Ephesus with St. John

The most blessed Mary, having enriched and blest Saragossa and the kingdom of Spain by her presence, and her promises of protection, and having established through St. James and her angels the church as a monument to her sacred name, was borne by the hands of the seraphim back to Jerusalem.

As soon as Queen of the angels left the cloud-throne, on which she had been borne, she set her foot upon the floor of the Cenacle, and prostrated Herself upon it, humbling herself to praise the Most High for the favors conferred upon her, upon St. James and upon the kingdom of Spain in this miraculous journey. The thought of a church built in her honor and for her invocation, in her humility, she entirely forgot that she was the Mother of God, a sinless Creature and without measure, superior to all the highest seraphim. She humbled Herself and gave thanks for these benefits.

In these exercises, and in praying with great fervor for the defense and increase of the Church, She spent the greater part of the four days after her return to Jerusalem. In the meanwhile the evangelist St. John made preparations for the journey to Ephesus, and on the fourth day, which was the fifth of January of the year forty, St. John notified Her that it was time to leave, for there would be a ship and all things had been arranged for the journey. She proceeded to take leave of the owner of the Cenacle and its inhabitants. The Blessed Mother thanked them and somewhat allayed their grief by giving them hope of her return.

For her greater alleviation and comfort during this journey all her holy angels on her leaving the Cenacle, appeared to Her in visible corporeal forms surrounding Her and protecting Her in their midst. With this escort of angels and the human company of St. John, they journeyed to the port, where the vessel was ready to sail for Ephesus.

They came to the harbor and immediately embarked in the ship with other passengers. For the Blessed Virgin Mary it was her first time upon the sea. She saw and comprehended with clearness the vast Mediterranean and its passage to the great ocean. She beheld its height and depth, its length and breadth, its caverns and secret recesses, its sands and minerals, its ebb and tide, its animals, its whales and fishes of all sizes, and whatever other animals it contained. She knew how many men had drowned and perished in voyaging it. Her knowledge extended to all these things not only as they are in themselves and without deceit, but far beyond the sphere of angelic knowledge.

166

With the compassion of a most loving Mother for those who trusted their lives to the indomitable fury of the sea in navigating over its waves, she most fervently besought the Almighty to protect from its dangers all who should call upon her name and ask for her intercession. The Lord immediately granted this petition and promised to favor whomever upon the sea should carry some image of Her and should sincerely look upon the Blessed Virgin Mary for help in its perils.

Another wonder also happened, for when the most blessed Mary saw the sea with the fishes and other marine animals, She gave them all her blessing and commanded them to acknowledge and praise their Creator in the manner they were capable of. Then it was wonderful to see all the fishes of the sea obeying her command and with incredible swiftness placing themselves in front of the ship. None of the species of sea animals was missing, each being represented by an innumerable multitude. All of them surrounded the ship and showed their heads above the water. This strange event astonished all the passengers as something never before seen. The multitudes of large and small fishes, so crowded and packed together, somewhat impeded the progress of the vessel, and the passengers gazed upon this spectacle in wonder and discussed it, for they did not know the cause of this miracle. St. John alone understood it. After some time he asked the heavenly Mother to give the marine creatures her blessing and her permission to depart since they had so promptly obeyed Her when asked to praise the Most High. The Blessed Mother complied, and immediately the great multitude of fishes disappeared and churned the sea into foam by their quick motion. Thereupon the ship pursued its way over the tranquil waters, arriving at Ephesus in a few days.

When they landed the Blessed Mother continued to work miracles equal to those wrought upon the sea. She cured the sick and the possessed, who, as soon as they came into her presence, were set free from the demons. In Ephesus lived some Christians, who had come from Jerusalem. The Blessed Virgin Mary chose for her dwelling the house of a few retired and poor women, who were living by themselves free from men.

By the intervention of the angels, they lovingly and generously placed their home at the disposition of the Lady. In it they selected a very secluded room for Mary and another for St. John, which these Two occupied during their stay in Ephesus.

The most blessed Mary thanked the owners, who were to live with Her. Then She retired to her room and prostrated herself upon the ground as was usual in her prayers. She continued her prayer for the holy Church and laid out her plans for the assistance of all the faithful from her room in Ephesus. She called her angels and sent some of them to aid the Apostles and disciples, whom She knew to be much oppressed by infidels and demons. Particularly, she provided assistance to St. Paul helping him out of difficult situations. She especially gave assurances to St. Peter, St. John, the other Apostles and disciples that Paul had indeed been miraculously converted by the Lord Jesus. And as a result they accepted St. Paul and praised God.

Learning that Herod had taken St. Peter prisoner in Jerusalem she prayed that the Lord Jesus would permit her to facilitate his release. The Lord Jesus joined her in this request and Both these Sovereigns ordered one of the angels there to go quickly to liberate Peter from his prison in Jerusalem. The angel executed these orders very swiftly. Coming to the dungeon, he found St. Peter fastened with two chains, guarded by two soldiers at his side and by a number of other soldiers at the entrance of the prison. The Passover had already been celebrated and it was the night before he was to be executed according to the sentence passed upon him. But the Apostle was sleeping as were his guards. When the angel arrived, he was obliged to wake him by force and while St. Peter was still drowsy, said to him: "Arise quickly! put on thy girdle and thy shoes, take thy mantle and follow me." St. Peter found himself free of the chains and, without understanding what was happening to him and ignorant of what this vision could mean, followed the angel. Having conducted him through some streets, the angel told him, that the Almighty had freed him from prison through the intercession of His most Blessed Mother, and thereupon disappeared.

St. Peter quickly went to the house of Mary, the mother of John, who was also called Mark. This was the house of the Cenacle, where many of the disciples had gathered in their affliction. Saint Peter called to them from the street, and a servant-maid, by the name of Rhode, descended to see who was calling. As she recognized the voice of Peter, she left him standing at the door outside and fled excitedly to the disciples, telling them that it was Peter. They thought it some foolish misunderstanding of the servant; but she maintained, that it was Peter, so they, far from guessing the liberation of Peter, concluded that it might be his angel. During these questions and answers St. Peter was in the street clamoring at the door, until they opened it and with incredible joy and gladness saw the holy Apostle and head of the Church freed from prison and death. He gave them an account of all that had happened to him through aid of the angel. Foreseeing that Herod would search for him with great diligence, they unanimously decided that he leave Jerusalem that very night and not return, lest he should be taken in some future search. Saint Peter therefore fled, and Herod, having instituted a search in vain, chastised the guards, and was roused to new fury against the disciples. But on account of his pride and impious designs, God cut short his activity by a severe punishment that would be executed by the Blessed Virgin Mary.

According to the Blessed Virgin Mary the gods of Egypt, Greece and Rome were real; they were Lucifer's top generals. Lucifer commanded these demons to befriend the humans so that by their own choice they would be condemned to hell and then in hell, the devils could torment them with the most horrific tortures for all eternity. The greatest temple of idolatry was the temple of Diana in Ephesus. The Blessed Virgin Mary inflamed with zeal for the honor of the Most High, commanded all the demons in the temple of Diana to descend immediately to the depths of hell and to leave the place which they had infested as their own for so many years. Many legions of them inhabited that temple, all of them were hurled into hell. And her angels destroyed the temple not leaving one stone upon another.

iii. The Blessed Virgin Mary executes Herod

[Editor's note: This is the only instance that a disagreement occurred between God the Blessed Virgin Mary.]

The Blessed Virgin Mary said to one of her seraphim: "I beseech thee to ascend to the throne of the Most High, represent to Him my affliction; ask Him in my name, that I may be permitted to suffer instead of his faithful servants and that Herod be prevented from executing his designs for the destruction of the Church." Immediately the angel betook himself to the Lord with this message.

The angel was sent back by the Blessed Trinity with the answer: "Princess of heaven, the Lord of hosts says, that Thou art the Mother and the Governess of the Church, and that Thou holds His power while Thou art upon earth, and He desires Thee, as the Queen of heaven and earth, to execute sentence upon Herod."

In her humility the Blessed Virgin Mary was somewhat disturbed by this answer, and she replied to the angel: "Am I then to pronounce sentence against a creature who is the image of the Lord? Since I came forth from His hands I have known many reprobates among men and I have never called for vengeance against them; but as far as I was concerned, always desired their salvation if possible, and never hastened their punishment. Return to the Lord, angel, and tell Him that my tribunal and power is inferior to and dependent upon His, and that I cannot sentence anyone to death without consulting my Superior, and if it is possible to bring Herod to the way of Salvation, I am willing to suffer … in order that this soul may not be lost." The angel hastened back with this second message of his Queen and having presented it before the throne of the most Blessed Trinity, was sent back to her with the following answer: "Our Queen, the Most High says, that Herod … is so obstinate in his malice, that he will take no admonition or instruction, he will not cooperate with the help given to him, nor will he avail himself of the fruits of the Redemption, nor of the intercession of the saints, nor of thy own efforts on his behalf."

For the third time the most holy Mary dispatched the angel with still another message to the Most High, saying: "If it must be that Herod die in order to hinder him from persecuting the Church, do thou, O angel, represent to the Almighty, … If then I am to be a loving Mother to men, who are the creatures of His hands and the price of His blood, how can I now be a severe judge against one of them? Never was I charged with dealing out justice, always mercy, to which all my heart inclines, and now it is troubled by this conflict of love with obedience to rigorous justice. Present anew, O angel, this my anxiety to the Lord, and learn whether it is not His pleasure that Herod die without my condemning him."

The holy angel ascended for the third time and the most Blessed Trinity listened to his message with the plenitude of pleasure and complacency at the pitying love of the Blessed Virgin Mary. Returning, the angel thus informed her: "Our Queen, Mother of our Creator and my Lady, the Almighty Majesty says that thy mercy is for those mortals who wish to avail themselves of thy powerful intercession, not for those who despise and abhor it like Herod, that Thou art the Mother of the Church invested with all the divine power, and that therefore it is meant Thou use it as is opportune, that Herod must die, but it shall be through thy sentence and according to thy order." The most blessed Mary answered: "Just is the Lord and equitable are his judgments. ... considering Herod having become an obstinate enemy of God, unworthy of his eternal friendship, by the most equitable justice of God, I condemn him to the death he has merited, in order that he may not incur greater torments by executing the evil he has planned." Making use of this power the Blessed Virgin Mary sent the angel to Csesarea, where Herod then was, to take away his life as the minister of divine justice. The angel executed the sentence without delay. The evangelist St. Luke says, that the angel of the Lord struck Herod and he was eaten up by worms. The wound of his stroke was interior and from it sprang the worms that ate his body from the inside to the outside.

24. Assumption of the Blessed Virgin Mary

Three days before the death of the Blessed Virgin Mary, the Apostles and disciples were gathered in Jerusalem and in the Cenacle. The first one to arrive was St. Peter, who was transported from Rome by the hands of an angel. At that place the angel appeared to him and told him that the passing away of the Blessed Virgin Mary was imminent and that God commanded him to go to Jerusalem in order to be present at that event. Thereupon the angel took him up and brought him from Italy to the Cenacle.

The Blessed Virgin Mary came to the entrance of her oratory in order to receive St. Peter. Then came St. Paul, to whom she showed the same reverence with similar tokens of her pleasure at seeing him. The Apostles saluted Her as the Mother of God, as their Queen of all Creation; but with a sorrow equal to their reverence, because they knew that they had come to witness her passing away. After these Apostles came the others and the disciples still living. Three days after, they were all assembled in the Cenacle. The heavenly Mother received them all with profound humility, reverence and love, asking each one to bless Her. All of them complied, and saluted Her with admirable reverence. By her orders given to St. John, and with the assistance of St. James his brother, they were all hospitably entertained and accommodated.

Some of the Apostles who had been transported by the angels and informed by them of the purpose of their coming, were seized with tender grief and shed abundant tears at the thought of losing their only protection and consolation. Others were as yet ignorant of their approaching loss, especially the disciples, who had not been positively informed by the angels, but were moved by interior inspirations and a sweet and forcible intimation of God s will to come to Jerusalem. They immediately conferred with St. Peter, desirous of knowing the occasion of their meeting; for all of them were convinced, that if there had been no special occasion, the Lord would not have urged them so strongly to come.

The apostle St. Peter, as the head of the Church, called them all together in order to tell them of the cause of their coming, and spoke to the assembly: "My dearest children and brethren, the Lord has called and brought us to Jerusalem from remote regions for a cause most urgent and sorrowful to us. The Most High wishes now to raise up to the throne of eternal glory his most blessed Mother, our Mistress, our consolation and protection. His divine decree is that we all be present at her most happy and glorious Transition. When our Master and Redeemer ascended to the right hand of his Father, although He left us orphaned of his most delightful presence, we still retained His Blessed Mother. As she now leaves us, what shall we do? What help or hope have we to encourage us on our pilgrimage? I find none except the hope that we all shall follow Her in due time."

St. Peter could speak no longer because uncontrollable tears interrupted him. Neither could the rest of the Apostles answer for a long time. After some time St. Peter recovered himself and added: "My children, let us seek the presence of our Blessed Mother and Lady. Let us spend the time left of her life in her company and ask Her to bless us." They all entered her room and found Her kneeling upon a couch, on which She wanted to recline for a short rest. They saw Her full of beauty and celestial light, surrounded by the thousand angels of her guard.

The natural condition and appearance of her sacred and virginal body were the same as at her thirty-third year as from that age onward it experienced no change. It was not affected by the passing years, showing no signs of age, no wrinkles in her face or body, nor giving signs of weakening or fading. Jesus along with many legions of angels came to be with His most Blessed Mother in her last hour. All of the angels began to sing in celestial harmony. Although only St. John and some of the Apostles were enlightened as to the presence of Jesus Christ the Savior, yet the others felt in their interior its divine and powerful effects; but the music was heard as well by the Apostles and disciples, as by many others of the faithful there present.

A divine fragrance also spread about, which penetrated even to the street. The house of the Cenacle was filled with a wonderful light, visible to all, and the Lord ordained that multitudes of the people of Jerusalem gathered in the streets as witnesses to these new miracles could smell the "odor of sanctity" and see the radiant light.

When the angels began their music, the most Blessed Mary reclined back upon her couch or bed. Her tunic was folded about her sacred body, her hands were joined and her eyes fixed upon her Divine Son, and She was entirely inflamed with the fire of divine love. She pronounced those words of her Son on the Cross: "Into Thy hands, O Lord, I commend my spirit." Then She closed her eyes and expired.

Then her most pure Soul passed from her virginal body to be placed in boundless glory, on the throne at the right hand of her Divine Son. Immediately the music of the angels seemed to withdraw to the upper air and a procession of angels and saints accompanied the King and Queen to the Empyrean Heaven. Still in the Cenacle the sacred body of the most Blessed Mary continued to shine with a radiant light and breathed forth such a wonderful and unheard of fragrance, that all the bystanders were filled with interior and exterior sweetness. The thousand angels of her guard remained to watch over her body still on earth. The Apostles and disciples, amid the tears and the joy of the wonders they had seen, were absorbed in admiration for some time, and then sang many hymns and psalms in honor of the most Blessed Mary now departed. This glorious Transition of the great Queen took place in the hour in which her divine Son had died, at three o'clock on a Friday, the thirteenth day of August, she being seventy years of age, less the twenty-six days intervening between the thirteenth of August, on which She died, and the eighth of September, the day of her birth. The heavenly Mother had survived the death of Christ the Savior twenty-one years, four months and nineteen days; and his virginal birth, fifty-five years.

This reckoning can be easily made in the following manner: when Christ our Savior was born, His virginal Mother was fifteen years, three months and seventeen days of age. The Lord lived thirty-three years and three months; so that at the time of his sacred Passion the most blessed Lady was forty-eight years, six months and seventeen days old ; adding to these another twenty-one years, four months and nineteen days, we ascertain her age as seventy years, less twenty-five or twenty-six days.*

*In figures as follows:
Birth of Jesus, Mary's Age: 15 years, 3 months, 17 days. Death of Jesus, Mary's Age: 48 years, 6 months, 17 days. Death of Mary, Mary's Age: 69 years, 11 months, 5 days.

Great miracles happened at the death of the Blessed Virgin Mary; the sun was eclipsed and its light was hidden for hours. Many birds of different kinds gathered around the Cenacle, and by their sorrowful clamors and groans for a while caused the bystanders themselves to weep. All Jerusalem was in commotion, and many of the inhabitants collected in astonished crowds, confessing loudly the power of God and the greatness of His works. Others were astounded and bewildered. The Apostles and disciples with others of the faithful broke forth in tears and sighs. Sick persons were cured. Souls in purgatory were released.

St. Peter called two maidens, who had assisted the Blessed Virgin Mary during her life and who had been designated as the heiresses of her tunics, and instructed them to anoint the body of the Mother of God with highest reverence and modesty and wrap it in the winding-sheets before it should be placed in the casket. With great reverence and fear the two maidens entered the room, where the body of the Blessed Virgin Mary lay upon her couch; but the radiance coming from it barred and blinded them in such a manner that they could neither see nor touch the body, nor even ascertain in what particular place it rested.

In fear and reverence still greater than on their entrance, the maidens left the room; and in great excitement and wonder they told the Apostles what had happened. They came to the conclusion, that the Blessed Virgin Mary was not to be touched in any way. Then St. Peter and St. John entered the oratory and saw the radiant light and smelled the fragrance and at the same time heard the celestial music of the angels, who were singing: "Hail Mary, full of grace, the Lord is with thee." From that time on many of the faithful expressed their devotion toward the Blessed Virgin Mary in these words of praise and from them they were handed down to be repeated by us with the approbation of the holy Church. The two holy Apostles, St. Peter and St. John, were for a time lost in admiration at what they saw and heard of their Queen; and in order to decide what to do, they sank on their knees, beseeching the Lord to make it known. Then they heard a voice saying: "Let not the sacred body be either uncovered or touched."

Having thus been informed of the will of God, they brought a bier, and, the radiance having diminished somewhat, they approached the couch and with their own hands reverently took hold of the tunic at the two ends. Thus, without changing its posture, they raised the sacred body and placed it on the bier in the same position as it had occupied on the couch. They could easily do this, because they felt no more weight than that of the tunic. On this bier the former radiance of the body returned more brilliant and by disposition of the Lord, all those present could now perceive and study the beauty of her face and of her hands. People brought many candles to be lighted at the bier, and it happened that all the lights burned through that day and the two following days without any of the candles being consumed or wasted in any shape or manner.
In order that the many miracles might become better known to the world, God Himself inspired all the inhabitants of Jerusalem to be present at the burial of His most Blessed Mother, so that all the occupants of Jerusalem were attracted by the novelty of this spectacle. The Apostles took upon their shoulders the sacred body in orderly procession from the Cenacle to the valley of Josaphat.

Also there was another invisible multitude of heavenly spirits. It was composed of the one thousand angels of the Queen, continuing their celestial songs, which were heard by the Apostles, disciples and others, that continued for three days. In addition, many legions of angels with the ancient Patriarchs and Prophets, were St. Joachim, St. Anne, St. Joseph, St. Elisabeth and St. John the Baptist and numerous saints, who were sent by our Savior Jesus to assist at the funeral and burial of His most Blessed Mother.

In the midst of this heavenly and earthly escort, visible and invisible, the Apostles bore along her sacred body, and on the way happened great miracles, which would take much time to mention, particularly all the sick were cured, the possessed were freed from the demons, for the evil spirits did not dare to wait until the sacred body came near the possessed persons. The miracles of conversions took place among many Jews and gentiles. The Apostles and disciples labored hard in catechizing and baptising those, who on that day had been converted to the holy faith. All the multitudes of the people were seized with astonishment at the fragrance (called "the odor of sanctity") diffused about, the sweet music and the other prodigies. They proclaimed God great and powerful in this Creature and in testimony of their acknowledgment, they struck their breasts. When the procession came to the holy sepulchre in the valley of Josaphat, the same two Apostles, St. Peter and St. John, who had placed the her from the couch onto the bier, with reverence placed her body in the sepulchre and covered it with a linen cloth, the hands of the angels performed more of these last rites than the hands of the Apostles. They closed up the sepulchre with a large stone, according to custom at other burials. The many legions of angels returned to heaven, while the one thousand angels of the Blessed Virgin Mary continued their watch, guarding her sacred body and keeping up the music as at her burial. As the crowd dwindled, the holy Apostles and disciples returned to the Cenacle.

Having again gathered in the Cenacle, the Apostles came to the conclusion that some of them and of the disciples should watch at the sepulchre of their Queen as long as they should hear the celestial music, for all of them were wondering when that miracle would end. Accordingly, some of them attended to the affairs of the Church in catechizing and baptizing the new converts, and others immediately returned to the sepulchre, while all of them paid frequent visits to it during the next three days. St. Peter and St. John, however, were more zealous in their attendance, coming only a few times to the Cenacle and immediately returning to where was laid the body of the Blessed Virgin Mary. When the time for her Assumption had arrived, Jesus Christ our Savior Himself descended from heaven bringing with Him at His right hand the soul of His most Blessed Mother and was accompanied by many legions of the Angels. Together they came to the sepulchre in the valley of Josaphat. At the command of the Lord Jesus, the soul of the Blessed Virgin Mary, entered her virginal body, reanimated it and raised it up, giving it a new life of immortality and glory and communicating to it the four gifts of clearness, impassibility, agility and subtlety, corresponding to those of the soul and overflowing from it into the body. Endowed with these gifts the most Blessed Virgin Mary came forth from the tomb in body and soul, without raising the stone cover and without disturbing the position of the tunic and the mantle that had enveloped her sacred body. Then from the sepulchre began a most solemn procession, moving with celestial music through the regions of the air and toward the empyrean heaven. This happened in the hour immediately after midnight, in which also the Lord Jesus had risen from the grave, and therefore not all of the Apostles were witness of this prodigy, but only those who were present and keeping watch at the sepulchre. The saints and angels entered heaven in the order in which they had started; and in then came Jesus our Savior and at his right hand the Blessed Virgin Mary. All of the angels and saints turned toward Her to look upon Her and bless Her with new songs of praise. Amid this glory the most Blessed Virgin Mary arrived body and soul at the throne of the most Blessed Trinity. And the Three Divine Persons received Her on it with an eternal embrace. …

25. Early Church v Modern Church Editor's Comments

Most Roman Catholics would agree that three of the greatest wonder working saints are: St Francis of Assisi, St Anthony of Padua, and St Pio of Pietralcina (aka Padre Pio).

Padre Pio was most famous for his ability as a confessor. Renown Catholic author Kenneth Woodward writes: "Padre Pio is credited with the gift of 'reading hearts'—that is, the ability to see into the souls of others and know their sins without hearing a word from the penitent. As his reputation grew, so did the lines outside his confessional—to the point that for a time his fellow Capuchins issued tickets for the privilege of confessing to Padre Pio." Whenever, Padre Pio administered Holy Communion or Baptism, a crucifix with Jesus on the cross would appear on his forehead.

St. Anthony of Padua performed numerous Eucharistic Miracles. St Francis of Assisi began the tradition of the Nativity Scene by having his village people build a stable and manger and bring a donkey, an ox and sheep on Christmas Eve. Then at midnight he called down from Heaven, the Baby Jesus, Mary & Joseph; a vision that the whole village witnessed. What did they all have in common? They were all Franciscans and as such they all took vows of poverty, chastity, and obedience.

The Blessed Virgin Mary has said that from the first Pentecost Sunday and throughout the early Church the spectacular "tongues of fire" descended from heaven and rested upon the heads of every believer that was receiving the Sacrament of Confirmation. And when any of the faithful recited the Apostles' Creed the Holy Spirit would visibly appear over their heads. Moreover, many miracles were visible when any of the 7 Sacraments were administered.*

*"The Mystical City of God" by Venerable Mary of Agreda, 1657. English translation in 1902 by Fiscar Marison, Volume IV, Chapter XIII, para 224 through 245.

What happened thereafter that caused God to abstain from blessing the administering of the 7 Sacraments with His magnificent spectacular miracles such as "tongues of fire"? In 312 Emperor Constantine was shown by God the cross and told "in this sign you will conquer". Constantine ordered his army to adorn their shields with the Christian symbol and was victorious at the Battle of Milvain Bridge which united his Empire and resulted in his conversion to Christianity. In the following year 313 Constantine issued his Edict of Milan which provided tolerance and protection of Christianity. The Roman Catholic Church considers the period of Christianity proceeding the First Council of Nicaea in 325 as "the early Church" aka "the primitive church". In 382 the Emperor Theodosius I with the Edict of Thessalonica declared Nicene Christianity (soon after called the Roman Catholic Church) the state church/religion of the Roman Empire.

Hence the Church was transformed from an impoverished, persecuted, outlawed, underground religion into a socially popular religion resulting in a very wealthy institution with tremendous political and military power.

Thus for 300 years, believers and nonbeliever witnesses were astonished and awestruck by spectacular visible phenomenon that came directly from the Most High Almighty God. And would no doubt be considered by all that were present as a Most Magnificent Divine Sign that God is pleased and bestowing His Sanctifying Grace on those receiving the holy sacraments. I can't imagine anyone then and now that would witness the "tongues of fire" descending from Heaven and resting on the heads of those being confirmed or just reciting the Apostles' Creed would have to have been converted at that very moment. For certain, witnessing this awesome spectacular visible sight had to spontaneously convert all nonbelievers and intensify the faith of believers. As a result, the Church grew very rapidly. Today as a result of secularism, the membership of the Church is diminished year after year; quite the opposite of the early Church.

Pope Francis chose his name from St Francis of Assisi. Obviously, the Holy Father significantly emulates St Francis. As such, he perhaps aspires to the virtues of St Francis. Recall the 1968 movie "The Shoes of the Fisherman" with Anthony Quinn as the Pope, who commits to dispense of all of the wealth of the Church to provide for the world's poor. Imagine, Pope Francis, overwhelmed by the spirit of St Francis of Assisi, compelled to dispense of the wealth of the Church to end global poverty. And since poverty is so immensely pleasing to Almighty God then it would be highly likely that the Church could expect a return to spectacular miracles such as the "tongues of fire" whenever any of the 7 Sacraments would be administered.

Moreover, miracles could be expected to accompany all 7 Sacraments as they did in the early Church in its first 300 years.

26. Lessons learned

• The Blessed Virgin Mary came first before the angels & man.

In His Infinite Wisdom, God knew the greatest love that could ever be is the love of a human Mother for her child and the love of a human child for his Mother. To experience this 'greatest love' was God's greatest desire. As such, the Onlybegotten Son of the Eternal Father would have to become Incarnate and born to a woman. As God is perfect, God's Mother has to be perfect. As God in the second person of the Blessed Trinity would become the "perfect man" then the Most High God would have to create the "perfect woman" e.g. Blessed Virgin Mary.

• God's Humility is the astonishment of the Angels.

The Angels knew that the Most High God could do all things. God can create and uncreate everything but the Angels were always in astonishment and completely surprised by the extent of God's humility.

• In the Eucharist the Eternal Father and the Holy Spirit are equally present with Jesus the Son.

This was agreed to by the Eternal Father at the 'Last Supper". From the creation of man the angels were greatly empathetic towards humanity as the angels felt that humans had significant disadvantages. But the empathy of the angels stopped at the institution of the Eucharist when they realized that they were disadvantaged because they did not have a physical body in order to receive the physical body of God.

• The majority of human race will be condemned to hell.

As one third of God's angels were lost, according to the Blessed Virgin Mary more than half of all of souls will be lost.

• There are 3 heavens.

According to the Blessed Virgin Mary, there are 3 heavens. The third heaven is the highest heaven the "Empyrean Heaven" which is the dwelling place of God and His Angels. Based on the editor's investigations, he has only found one situation where Jesus guarantees entry into the Empyrean Heaven. And that is "The Fifteen Prayers of Love & Gratitude to Jesus Crucified" given to St. Bridgette of Sweden to be prayed everyday for one year to honor each of Jesus' 5,480 wounds.

• "My God, My God, why have you forsaken me?" = The only disagreement to ever occur between the Father and the Son.

The Onlybegotten Son was forsaken (disagreed) by the Eternal Father only one time. Jesus' argument was equitable; as all of the human race were condemned by the action of one man, then all of the human race should be redeemed by the action of one man. But the Eternal Father would only allow for redemption to apply to those that accept Jesus as their Saviour and followed His teachings.

• Guardian Angels

The guardian angels are elevated and receive rewards determined by the spiritual achievements of the human beings that are in their charge.

• What angers God the most?

1) Ingratitude
The Blessed Virgin Mary states that if anyone goes more than one hour without expressing gratitude to God they will risk being guilty of serious sin.

2) Hopelessness
God is most angry when people express hopelessness, especially after He has made the Blessed Virgin Mary a Sovereign of the universe giving her equal power to Himself and allowing her complete discretion to distribute mercy and

183

justice as she should see fit to all that call upon her.
To that regard she taught Sister Mary of Agreda the following prayer:

"The Lord Jesus is my light, my life and my salvation, of whom should I fear. The Most High God is my friend and my helper, why should I worry. I have a Mother, the Mother of God. I have a Queen, the Queen of Angels. I have a Sovereign Lady; that God has elevated and given her power equal to His Own. By her Maternal Love and Protection, she will assist me in all my afflictions."

3) Hatred
The sin of Satan is hatred. No one is allowed into the Empyrean Heaven, God's dwelling place, with hatred in their heart.

● The Last Secret of Faith

The Blessed Virgin Mary was taken up to the Empyrean Heaven with Jesus at the Ascension. After she prostrated herself before the throne of God, the Eternal Father picked her up and placed her on the throne of the Blessed Trinity and made her a Sovereign of the universe and gave her equal powers to His own. Although she was bilocated to heaven for three days, she was more in Heaven than on earth. According to God, He was completely satisfied with her life, so He left it up to her decision to either stay in Heaven or return to earth. She chose to stay on earth to be the Mother of the new faith and provide her assistance for thirty-three more years.

Made in the USA
Columbia, SC
23 November 2024

47318165R00114